THE INVESTING KING

How I Started Angel Investing
with $25,000, Found the Next
Billion-Dollar Startups, and You
Can Too.

ROSS D. BLANKENSHIP

(CEO, AngelKings.com)

With Eugene H. Chung

THANK YOU

I'm so thankful to the family and friends who make what I do - finding, investing and building America's next top startups - possible.

My main inspirations are my brilliant wife and our two daughters — Jackson and Lily - who make me laugh, sing, dance, and smile every day.

It's for the generations before me who paved this uncommon path.

It's for the infinite wisdom of the beautiful Latin words, "Tempus Fugit." That time flies... which is indeed true and makes my days that more fulfilling in anticipation when there are no days left.

Because investing in startups is like burying your hard-earned dollars in the middle of a dry field, hoping one day that those dollars will grow into a rain forest where the money's flowing rapidly and the ecosystem is blossoming. Though it might seem impossible that a dry field could become an arid landscape, beneath every surface, I look for the real oil, energy, and infinite possibilities for a new Amazon to grow.

It takes a phenomenal amount of faith and perseverance - and setbacks - to reach success. And without family and friends along the way - even those who are often unable to describe what I do or even those who have called me crazy for what I do - it wouldn't be as fun climbing the trees of the forests I've built, without these friends and family.

There are also people I'd like to thank for helping make this book happen. Major appreciation goes to Eugene Chung. As a recent graduate of Duke University, and one who neither shies from risk nor is afraid of the unknown... I'm lucky to have found you. We met in the most unconventional way - not through a boring job board - but rather because we share a passion for risk, adventure, and the love of helping others. So glad our paths crossed and for what potential the future holds.

Thank you to the investors at Angel Kings Investment Group, which continues to grow every year.

Also, thank you to Chris Park, who helped with last minute editing and guidance on our book.

And even though I continue to tell my brother, Michael J. Blankenship, so many times about futuristic concepts like Ethereum, Blockchain, and the many startups I help, he's finally starting to see the upside! For that, he will be thankful.

This book is a collection of the infinite wisdom I've learned from the amazing people with whom I surround myself.

Thank you all.

Now, let's go find the next great startups together.

*To learn about Angel Kings, and one of our startup and venture capital funds, visit <u>AngelKings.com</u> today.

The Investing King

TABLE OF CONTENTS

PREFACE

Why did I write a book about investing, startups, and how investors need to think differently if they want to beat the stock market's returns? Why am I releasing my investing formula to the public, for the first time?

After all, there are so many authors and investing experts who believe their formula for success is better than his or her predecessor. But the story about why I became known as the "Investing King" and why I wrote this book is rooted in one conversation, that happened not too long ago.

In the summer of 2016, a Bloomberg reporter called me to talk about my experience as one of the first investors in a currency called "Ethereum." Also known as "Ether" or "ETH," the reporter was curious how and why I began accumulating this novel currency. She had heard about some of my previous investments, and was curious why I would be, "inclined to do such a thing?" At the time, one Ether ("ETH") was trading for about $7 per coin.

The Ethereum Network and many of the first exchange platforms had been hacked, numerous times. There were naysayers and "tulip" bubble talkers everywhere. Ethereum, people surmised, would fall to nothing; it was all just a temporary blip, and businesses would go on without using this smart-contract technology. But, as always, I looked beyond the hype, beyond the negativity, and searched for real buy signals within this noise.

Notably, as the chief rival to Bitcoin, Ethereum's possibilities in the developer world – allowing a decentralized framework

– for applications and programs to be built with speed and efficiency. A revolutionary currency that no doubt has the potential to be what the Internet protocol in the 1980s and 1990s would become.

The number of Ethereum developers who were meeting up to discuss this virtual currency and the decentralized network had expanded from 1,000 per month to more than 100,000 per month within six months.

Transaction volume on the Ethereum network had hockey-stick, exponential growth. The brilliant mind behind Ethereum - Vitalik Buterin - was remarkable. I saw that he could quickly become an icon within the industry. Ethereum as a "product" had the potential to disrupt every corner of the financial markets, Internet of Things (IoT) networks, and large corporate intermediaries who are building new products from ID verifications to stock exchanges. There was traction. There was momentum. Adoption of this technology was rapid, but as always, I looked beyond the headlines. I showed up to the meetings. Interviewed many key Ethereum individuals, and even invested in emerging platforms based on Ethereum such as Numer.ai – a hedge fund where Ethereum was the currency of exchange that rewarded data scientists for accurate stock market predictions.

Bottom line: I did my homework, and then went above and beyond.

In fact, I never invest unless I can explain the concept, the product, and talk about the founders fluently, and with a passion for what they're building.

I explained what I mentioned above to the reporter as my reasons for investing, but when she asked me why again, I responded immediately that these five principles guide every one of my investments: **People, Product, Process, Traction,** and **Financials**.

It doesn't matter what technology or "Next Big Thing" comes along. If you want to break down the hysteria, hype, and mystery, and decide whether the investment opportunity is right for you: be consistent and use the newly-released formula in this book – **"The Blankenship Valuation Method."**

These five factors had served me well investing in the next great companies with examples such as Buffer, Unsplash, and Managed by Q, so how on earth could the same principles be applied to this novel "crypto-currency?"

The answer was, and is, simple: at the heart of every new technology and of every future "great" technology, these five principles remain the most important and common motif – DNA – that embodies what it takes to go from a mere startup to a mega-empire, billion-dollar business.

Now many of my investments are focused on biotech and cybersecurity. But I've proven many times that the Blankenship Valuation Method is agnostic; it's a formula that is fully-applicable to any industry, vertical or market approach.

In the past ten years, I've learned that every startup, every company – small, medium or large – is fundamentally the same. Though they may have different products or services, what makes them win or lose is all shared in the five principles of a startup's DNA.

I always look past the hype and the pompous circumstances of promoters, and retain key principles that have guided me to 10x, 100x and greater returns – not always – but frequently enough that I can do venture capital full-time. And I'm 100% confident that after reading this book, watching our course (AngelKings.com/Course), and investing in yourself through many of the free resources on our site (AngelKings.com/Advisors), that you too can become an expert in the field, even if you can't be full-time or quit your job.

Fundamentally, I believe every investor and entrepreneur deserves to know what challenges they're up against and what opportunities exist along the way.

Every investor deserves a piece of the multi-trillion-dollar world of venture capital and startups.

So, I'll show you too how to ask the right questions of a potential investment, how to invest just enough that if you lost the money, you wouldn't be financially devastated, but enough money that if you had a 100x return, you could retire a few years early.

I'll show you how to be objective, not subjective in your approach to investing; how to remove your gut feeling, and replace it with calculated-risk taking.

I'll even show you what will become the next billion and trillion-dollar opportunities within the world of angel investing, venture capital, and startups.

Whether you're an investor in search of the next billion-dollar company – the next Apple, Facebook, Google, Microsoft, or Uber – and need guidance to help better understand and parse the noise from the signal within investing, this book goes beyond basic investing advice and gets to the heart of what makes successful companies tick, every day.

Whether you're an entrepreneur seeking investment capital, funding, or a better way to understand the term sheet, hiring, and operational management, or just ways to connect with investors, like me, get ready to have everything you know about startups analyzed and parsed for the most important things you need to know.

In this book, I'm formally introducing the Blankenship Valuation Method to the public. Having applied my valuation principles to more than 40+ companies – with many big liquidity events and exits – I think it's time for you to get this insider knowledge too. You deserve it.

And the good news is that you can apply the Blankenship Valuation Method to any new or future investment model – in the private and public markets – as all successful startups share common threads that when present can create mega-winners, but without which a startup either becomes a lifestyle (non-investable entity), or a failure.

After reading my book, taking the course, and asking me questions via e-mail (invest@angelkings.com) or via Twitter (@RossBlankenship), I will show you how to become a winning, profitable investor.

Let's all start making more money by investing in America's next top startups, together.

Ross D. Blankenship
CEO | AngelKings.com
invest@angelkings.com

******

*BONUS RESOURCES FOR YOU:

Before beginning this book, be sure to enroll in our popular,
on-demand startup course:

AngelKings.com/Course

And if you ever need help growing your startup or existing
business, be sure to connect with our team:

AngelKings.com/Advisors

1

Introduction

"It is our choices... that show what we truly are, far more than our abilities."

-J.K. Rowling

Are You Ready to Change Your Life With Angel Investing?

Everyone thinks you need millions of dollars to begin angel investing. However, I turned a small sum of $25,000 into a venture capital firm that has invested in startups now worth billions. Want to know a secret about this success? You can do it, too. This book will give you everything you need to know to start investing right away. New investors often don't know where to start or what to look for. However, I'll teach you which characteristics make effective startups, so you can succeed in your investing goals.

Consider this: over the last decade angel investors and venture capitalists have collectively invested over $500 billion dollars in startups. That amount is greater than the GDP of an entire nation like Poland or Belgium. However, not all investors have been successful. Those that failed chose to go off their gut feeling rather than using objective, valuable information to justify their decisions. Of the millions of investors writing checks each year, some have had success, but most could have done better. If they had known what I know now, and what you're about to learn, the value and returns of their investment dollars could have been much greater.

But How Much Can You *Really* Make?

When you know what you're doing with angel investing and venture capital, you can see big gains that continue to build over time. The average return for a venture capital firm over the past decade was 15% higher than the portfolio of the average investor. Are you average? I'll bet you're not, which is why I will show you how to make the investing decisions you might be considering. If you think your investment portfolio is not performing well, or you're envious of all the high-dollar returns your friend, colleague, or neighbor is collecting, now's your chance to change your life.

As the Founder and CEO of Angel Kings, I've been part of many successful startups both as an investor and as an entrepreneur. Let me tell you, the path hasn't been easy.

To give you an example of my startup hustle, in the early 2000s, I balanced a full-time NCAA Division one sport, Varsity Rowing, while tutoring more than 22 students in math. This hustle allowed me to pay for my first online website projects. Every day at Cornell University, I worked from 5 a.m. until midnight either taking the maximum number of course credits, rowing on the Cayuga Inlet, or building my first business. Having this hard work ethic allowed me to raise enough money to pay for law school.

During my law school days at Washington University School of Law, I envisioned many of the most innovative technologies that have shaped the past decade including online learning, digital currencies and the Blockchain, and mobile cybersecurity. One idea imagined was the concept called "text-to-login" technology, but better known as "Multi-

Factor Authentication." At its core, this technology allows you to log in securely by receiving a one-time code from your mobile phone. It was an amazing concept. But in order for it to work and gain widespread adoption, I knew it needed to be simple and easy for consumers to understand. I also knew with the rapid advancement of mobile phones that the need to protect consumers on their mobile devices would be critical, and thus I went searching for startups solving these problems.

Find the Problem, Then Build the Solution

Along with studying, learning, and writing about new technology, I was in constant search for startups whose product fit my vision. In fact, I was able to invest early in a company called "Authy," which happened to be building the perfect product for mobile cybersecurity.

My earliest investment, Authy would eventually be acquired by a larger company called Twilio (Ticker: TWLO), a multi-billion-dollar, publicly-traded IPO. And that's just *one* example out of nearly 40 companies in which I've studied, learned about, wrote about, and invested in during the earliest rounds as an angel investor.

While dreaming up innovative technologies, I also built my education business from the ground up (from 1 to 250 people), and accelerated my technology consulting and education business, concurrently. Along each step of the way, I faced competition with massive budgets and workforces with hundreds of thousands of people versus my practice of building lean startups with just the right number of people. But my biggest achievement wasn't launching my business as a teenager; it has always been learning from every obstacle and making less mistakes on each new journey.

I have always been a visionary with the future of technology; this has allowed me to earn the name "The Investing King." I can spot new technologies easily ("Veni"), I can see the future beyond the clichés and trends ("Vidi"), and I am then able to capture on these ideas and execute by creating a monopoly ("Vici").

Now I'm going to share with you the secret lessons I've learned about the world of venture capital and startups so you can conquer these new technologies on your own and become the next Investing King, or Queen. This is exclusive information that will help you become part of the future of technology and reap the rewards of investing in it. I have founded successful companies, and also invested in the cybersecurity, e-commerce, and biotech sectors. Many of these are billion-dollar companies now, but they weren't when they started.

What if you had the chance to spot the next billion-dollar company before they launched, just like I did?

What if you had the opportunity to invest in a company long before it went public?

Now you do.

rno 70 poly

Can You Show Me How to Master the Art of Investing?

Absolutely. In this book, I'll show you how to use my formulas, insights, and the "Blankenship Valuation Method" that I've created. By using my formula, you'll obtain game-winning adjustments to your portfolio. You'll begin to watch your portfolio climb higher every year, and reap the benefits of knowing how to invest the right way. You'll not only learn what the Blankenship Valuation Method is, but also how to get started investing, how to look at valuations, and how to spot the next billion-dollar company. This proprietary formula will make you more money than investing in the public markets. This method offers a 100-point scale, and it will guide you through five steps that make investing and entrepreneurship foolproof.

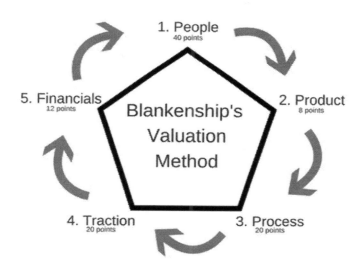

People, product, process, traction, and the financials are all assigned points under my valuation method. This gives you a way to measure a company objectively, and to stop investing based on your "gut" feelings. You want to temper those feelings with objective information that can help ensure that you're doing the right thing. Even if you like someone personally, you should always choose competency over loyalty. Using a competent method will help prevent investment failure. This book will give you the tools you need to value companies the right way.

While reading this book, use the formula above as a reference point and refer back to it before you make any investing decisions. The primary goal of this formula is to help you master the art of investing by creating an evaluation and metrics-driven process that replaces intuition with logic and reason.

But How Much Money Should You Invest?

If you're looking to beat the markets long-term or maybe just your neighbor next door, here's the perfect, **Blankenship Portfolio Allocation** that will allow you to reach the mega-returns of top startup investors and venture capitalists:

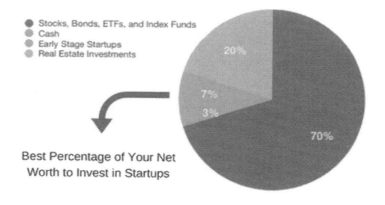

Blankenship Portfolio Allocation

- Stocks, Bonds, ETFs, and Index Funds
- Cash
- Early Stage Startups
- Real Estate Investments

Best Percentage of Your Net Worth to Invest in Startups

20%

7%

3%

70%

Yes, that's correct. Plan on allocating up to 7% of your entire investing portfolio if you want to see returns of the most successful angel investors and venture capitalists in the world. In fact, we've found that this allocation works for people in their 30s as much as it does for people in their 60s. Be willing to use the Blankenship Valuation Method, find the next billion-dollar startups, and put your money where your mouth is by investing 7% of your portfolio for potentially massive returns within venture capital.

To Summarize, Here's What This Book Will Show You:

Entrepreneurs will learn:

(1) What investors want to see when you pitch the idea and vision for your startup.
(2) How to raise both venture capital and angel investments to get your startup launched and ready for the big league.
(3) How to structure your startup for success in legal, financial, and operational matters.
(4) What you should be looking for in financials and startup valuations.
(5) The importance of startups achieving profits in just a year's time.

Investors will gain valuable knowledge and insight on:

(1) The future of investing in technology and how to spot the next billion-dollar ideas.
(2) Examples of startups that were once small ideas that became major success stories.
(3) How to get started investing, including the red flags and caveats you need to be aware of before writing your first check.
(4) How to look at valuations, financials, and investment sizes for startups, no matter what level of investor you are.
(5) How to handle due diligence and background research without feeling overwhelmed by legal and financial terms.

***

Now, we start with the most important factor in the Blankenship Valuation Method, the **People**...

2

People
The Founding Team

"People work better when they know what the goal is and why. It is important that people look forward to coming to work in the morning and enjoy working."

-Elon Musk

The Lifeblood of Each and Every Startup

The most important aspect to consider when investing in any startup is the founding team. A company without a good founder is not going to go very far. When you are writing your first check to a startup, you are not only investing in the company but also in the people who operate and believe in the company. You are investing in those people's ideas, goals, and dreams. If you do not believe that their ideologies are worth supporting financially, investing in that company is not the right choice. Therefore, it is crucial for you to understand exactly which traits you are searching for and identify the right people whose values align with yours.

Since the quality of a startup's "People" has the greatest impact on the success of a company, the Blankenship Valuation Method evaluates it first and gives it the greatest weight out of the five stages. 40 out of the maximum 100 points can possibly be attained here.

ributed through seven questions. Here are
ınt questions you need to ask startup

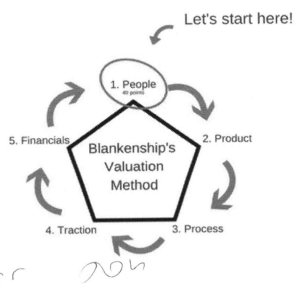

Let's start here!

1. People
40 points

5. Financials

Blankenship's
Valuation
Method

2. Product

4. Traction

3. Process

1. Are the founders of the startup fully committed and working on it full-time? (15 pts.)
2. Do the founding members look like the best possible combo? (15 pts.)
3. How many of the original founders stayed to continue working on the startup? (2 pts.)
4. Do any of the founders have the potential to become icons that can stand out to the public? (2 pts.)
5. Are the founders experienced in managing their finances? (2 pts.)
6. Would you trust the founders with a blank check upon conducting a credit and background check? (2 pts.)
7. Are the founders responsive to your ideas? (2 pts.)

I will use this section to describe the composition of a successful founding team, the qualities necessary to become an iconic leader, and ways to find people with that potential.

What Ingredients Does a Startup Need to Be Successful?

Three types of people are necessary for a successful startup, and only having one or two of them is not going to be reliable enough for investors. However, it does not mean that three people are required to operate the startup. Sometimes, it is better to have just one or two co-founders. If one person can effectively serve two roles, there is nothing wrong with that as long as the ability to do so is there. The three types of people that are imperative in a successful founding team are the "Hacker", "Hustler", and "Growth Hacker".

In the above visual, Kristin is the Growth Hacker; she is savvy with social media and is the storyteller of the company. Robert is the Hustler; he is good with people and can procure new customers. Melissa assists with organization and ensures that all jobs are being completed. David is the "All-Around", multifaceted person who can fill any role in the case of an emergency or member absence. Sam is the Hacker; he is the core engineer and is capable of coding, creating, and developing the product.

Enter: the "Hacker"

Hacker = Coder, Builder, Core Engineer

A Hacker is required for any successful startup. A Hacker is the core engineer, responsible for coding and building the product. The biggest concern with not having a Hacker is that you are unable to create the proper structure and framework necessary for the company to start. Although the role may be outsourced, outsourcing it creates two problems. First, it costs a lot of money that the startup likely does not have. Second, it implies that the people who are starting the company are incapable of building the product, and thus, if the hired developer does poorly or leaves, they will be unable to easily continue. The lapse of continuity caused by the latter will be more damaging than the former, but both are serious issues.

Let's use Facebook as an example. Mark Zuckerberg, who is the Founder and CEO, began his company at Harvard. Unlike the Winklevoss twins who tried to create a similar product and attempted to hire a developer, Zuckerberg built and created his product in-house with his roommate, Dustin Moskovitz. The two of them were the initial Hackers and product builders for Facebook. Although it is difficult to find the next Zuckerberg and Moskovitz, your search for the next billion-dollar founders will be easier upon following the Blankenship Valuation Method's principles.

Dustin Moskovitz (left) and Mark Zuckerberg (right)

Don't Forget About That Hustle!

Hustler = Sales Phenom, Builder of Rapport, Customer Engineer

Hustlers are also necessary in successful startups. They are knowledgeable in procuring new customers. You are looking for a personable individual who can handle sales at both the B2B (business-to-business) and B2C (business-to-consumer) levels. The person should be able to charm nearly everyone, have a good rapport with people in all levels of society, and have some understanding of the features that require custom engineering in order to keep the largest number of customers happy. The Hustler's main focus is to bring in many consumers in the most cost-effective way possible. If the person is incapable of doing so, he or she is not as effective as the person needs to be.

Eduardo Saverin is one of the co-founders and the first CFO of Facebook, and later became a successful Internet entrepreneur and angel investor. He met Zuckerberg at Harvard, and they aspired to create a social network for college students. Saverin was the president of the Harvard Investment Association, and his strong background in economics helped him lead Facebook's business development. His charm helped gain users and earned him the title of Facebook's Hustler.

We have covered two of the three key roles of a successful founding team. Now, let's talk about the Growth Hacker.

Eduardo Saverin

The Growth Hacker - The Story Teller

Growth Hacker = In-House, Crafter of the Narrative, Story-teller and Sharer

Lastly, the Growth Hacker is vital to a startup's success and longevity. The Growth Hacker is a storyteller who can craft a good narrative for the company and tell that story to the general public via the Internet and social media. He or she needs to not only have a strong understanding of the most standard and largest social media platforms like Facebook, Twitter, and Instagram, but also of software (e.g. Buffer) that controls which messages and company narratives get released to the public. If he or she can efficiently and eff... manage those platforms, the company has a better chance getting past the startup stage and consequently increasing the profit of your investment.

Christopher Hughes gained the role of being Facebook's Spokesperson – and Growth Hacker – after he made valuable product suggestions, most notably the idea of closed school networks to maintain more intimate environments. He engaged with customers and led marketing to help Facebook grow into what it is today.

Chris Hughes

Zuckerberg, Moskovitz, Saverin and Hughes all met in college and created Facebook, which is now worth more than $500 billion dollars. The founding team had the three important roles (Hacker, Hustler, and Growth Hacker) filled from its earliest days.

Since you now understand what to look for in a great founding team, the next step is to focus on finding founders who have the potential to become icons generally recognized by the public. The following section will highlight the ideal makeup of a billion-dollar founder.

If the Public Forgets the Founder, They Forget the Company

Founders need to possess certain qualities that make them memorable. Two great examples are Steve Jobs and Elon Musk. They are iconic. People know who they are, and they stand out. Their uniqueness and drive are important and

d. When you are deciding whether or not a part of a startup, you should identify founders possess similar qualities to Jobs are easily explained with our "**PACED**"

Steve Jobs (left) and Elon Musk (right)

All Founders Should PACED Themselves

Passionate = Key to Driving the Narrative
Ambivert = Better than Extroverted
Calculated Risk Taker = Fears Inaction
Erudite = Always Learning and seeking knowledge
Dedicated = All-In in the Pursuit of Success

PACED - Passionate

The founder of any startup needs to be passionate about what he or she is doing. The person needs to create and drive a narrative, and that narrative needs to matter. Does your founder have an underdog story? Is he or she a dropout genius? A challenger of the system or a rebel with a serious cause? Regardless of who is the founder, he or she needs to embrace that narrative and mold it into the startup's identity. People will remember the story and subsequently remember the company. It is cost-free advertisement and marketing. The founder's narrative makes a significant difference in how people react to the company during its earlier stages, which could then affect the longevity and ability to become more than just a startup.

A startup can soar when the media becomes obsessed with its founder. However, that could also become a problem if the founder does not portray exemplary qualities. Startup founders who get into serious trouble will damage their personal reputation and business. Therefore, it is imperative for potential investors in startups to search for founders who are memorable and have clean backgrounds. If the founder's passion is unable to be properly conveyed, the public will not respond to the startup in the manner that the investors and the company may have hoped for.

You should want passionate people in the startup because they are easily remembered. For example, Elon Musk has invested his time and effort in PayPal, Tesla, and SpaceX along with many other companies. He is a

Ross' Lesson: find founders whose personal narrative will help sell the company and its products to investors and customers.

paradigm of someone who is passionate and purposeful. The companies that he created and poured his passion into have changed the financial and transportation industries.

Musk sought to create a new payments system for billions of people worldwide through PayPal. Then, he founded Tesla, predicting that the era of green energy technology was approaching, and revolutionized the transportation industry. Steve Jobs was another founder who was passionate and worked with a sense of purpose. He was adopted by Syrian parents and experienced a difficult childhood, including frequent bullying from his peers. He fell in love with computers when he was twelve years old and knew by high school that he wanted to work with something involving them. He attended Reed College but dropped out to fully focus on creating Apple. During Apple's infancy, Jobs constantly shared his story with the media, making them aware of his background. The media began to obsess and publish pieces that crafted Jobs as a "dropout genius." Having someone who has a compelling story like Jobs at the helm of a startup allows the media to remain interested in what the company is doing. That is important because a strong narrative attracts attention, which in turn establishes a brand following and increases revenue.

PACED - Ambivert

Most people have heard of introverts and extroverts but probably not about ambiverts. Ambiverts possess a combination of both introverted and extroverted personality types, which is the most ideal for a successful business. They are not only good listeners. They talk enough when necessary and are not too reserved to lead effectively while making their voices heard. Both Steve Jobs and Elon Musk fit the ambivert description. Neither was overly extroverted but both had the talent of speaking to large groups about the things that they found interesting.

Ross' Lesson: ambiverts tend to sell the most. Make sure you pick them over extroverts.

Ambiverts may also be difficult to read, and they are nonconformists. That could be a good and bad thing, so it is important to watch over them carefully. Still, ambiverts are the types of people you want operating any startup that you are going to invest in. Although ambiverts may be difficult to notice in a room, they are easily identifiable when their presence brightens up as they converse about their niche, industry, or passions. At their core, ambiverts understand when to speak and when to listen.

Ambiverts care about what is changing around the world, so they stay ahead of the curve and always study what they can do differently. They are always on the cutting edge as early adopters of technology and current trends. Although they think deeply and do not usually have a lot to say, they want to share their gifts, talents, and information with others. Therefore, try to find more ambiverts when you consider which people to invest in or hire.

PA<u>C</u>ED – Calculated Risk Taker

People who are risk-takers may go too far and harm their own efforts, but people who do not take any risks may experience stagnation. That is why I always prefer calculated risk-takers as founders of startups. You need to find people who both fear inaction and are cautious with their actions. Those are the people who make startups move and ensure that the risks taken have the highest chance of benefitting everyone involved. They do this through several methods, including lagging behind the market just enough to check for viability.

Ross' Lesson: the fear of inaction is the greatest reason startups fail.

Successful founders are generally not the first to market something new because they wait for products that have a proven demand. When they identify that there is indeed a demand, they are quick to enter the marketplace with another, hopefully improved, version of the product. They also put at least some of their personal money into the startup, recognizing the value of what they are doing and being willing to invest in it. Although they are not afraid of failure, they are afraid of doing nothing and letting everything pass by them. Failure is sometimes required, and it becomes a valuable lesson.

When Elon Musk started SpaceX, he had to compete against many private companies. He encountered repeated resistance whenever he launched new products, and he was not the first one in the market. When Steve Jobs began the Apple brand, he had to overcome countless failures. In January 1983, he launched LISA, which failed completely. Then, in 1985, he was fired as Apple's CEO. However, they did not see those issues as failures but as minor roadblocks instead. True leaders look for ways to maneuver and overcome obstacles. By doing so, they avoid failing and learn much more about themselves, the world, and what it takes to be successful in business.

PAC<u>E</u>D – Erudite

When you look for startup founders, look for knowledge seekers. People who want to learn and develop are going to be much more dedicated to the company than those who are not passionate and are simply in it for the money. Your founders should be erudite, well-read and have tremendous knowledge on the subject. They should be ready and willing to learn as much as they can because there is always something new to learn. They should also want to exchange knowledge with other people and see the importance in doing so for their future.

Erudite and dedicated startup founders should be aware of the literature currently available in their subject niche and be people who would someday write a book on the topic despite it already existing on the market. They understand what they need to say, the knowledge that they could offer, and what the world needs to learn about their industry.

A founder has a higher chance of being ready, willing, and able to get his or her company off the ground if he or she has more wisdom to offer. Both Musk and Jobs are thought leaders and experts who share knowledge and educate others on their respective niches. Elon Musk is a thought leader in the finance and transportation industry while Steve Jobs was one in the technology industry. Erudite leaders are excited to share with the rest of the world the knowledge that they diligently sought out and gained.

Ross' Lesson: founders who are knowledge seeking, or "erudite," are always better coaches and trainers to the employees who then make a company successful.

PACE**D** – Dedicated

Dedication is a pivotal trait for a startup's founder. It will be a bad choice for angel investors and venture capitalists to invest in founders who treat their startups as part-time gigs. You need to invest in people who are 100% committed to winning. If you are an entrepreneur, you need to be all-in on your company. That is how you make a startup work and how you get people to invest in your beliefs. Think about it this way: why should investors believe in the startup and entrust large sums of money if the founders do not believe in the company enough to work full-time on it?

Elon Musk understood what it meant to be dedicated when he worked on PayPal and his other ventures. He worked day and night, and in many cases, even slept in his office. His vision was bigger than worrying about getting enough sleep, going out and having fun, or spending time at home. What mattered to Musk was the dream he envisioned in front of him, and he was not going to let anything prevent him from pursuing it to its fullest extent.

Ross' Lesson: invest in founders that are 100% dedicated to working full time on their companies.

Elon Musk has all the characteristics of our **PACED** acronym. Regardless of whether it was PayPal, SpaceX, or Tesla, he succeeded in growing the company and revolutionizing the respective industry. When looking at startups to invest in, it is important to evaluate the people who run the startup. The founder must be passionate and dedicated to the company. He or she needs to not only listen well, but also be able to enthusiastically discuss subjects that concern him or her. That person should be afraid of inaction, willing to take calculated risks, and eager to learn. Since "People" are the most important aspect when investing in a startup, it is essential to ensure that the founder exhibits all of the qualities associated with PACED.

Where Can You Find the Next Mark Zuckerberg?

Finding good founders does not have to be a difficult process. First, there are particular locations to consider. Two of the best places to look for founders are technology startup incubators and college campuses. If you focus on those places, you will have a higher chance of encountering people who are serious about what they are doing and understand the value of their work. At tech incubators, founders come together for a six to twelve-week period, launch startups during that time, and present their products at the end during a "demo day." It is a great way to see the ideas that people have and how they can bring those ideas to life.

College campuses contain many of the next generation's thought leaders. Yes, there are plenty of students who are only concerned with obtaining a degree and perfectly content working for someone else. However, in addition to those students, there are others who are focused on conducting personal research, publishing papers, and much more. You should target and connect with those people because they place value in other aspects besides simply getting a degree. They want to change the world, and their goals may very well come into fruition if they stay dedicated and receive some financial funding.

When you discover potential founders, do not forget to use the **Blankenship Valuation Method**. Even if something sounds like the next greatest idea, it is critical to be aware of potential issues that may arise. If you can take into account more issues, your evaluation of the product will be significantly greater. The Blankenship Valuation Method will help mitigate any risk and better determine whether or not the startup is worth your investment. Just ensure that any founding team you consider has people responsible for the three main roles (Hacker, Hustler, Growth Hacker) because that makes or breaks the startup. Without people to fill those roles, the probability of success tremendously diminishes.

Conclusion

Let's reintroduce the Blankenship Valuation Method and reflect on the startup DNA that will help you find winning founders and future success stories…

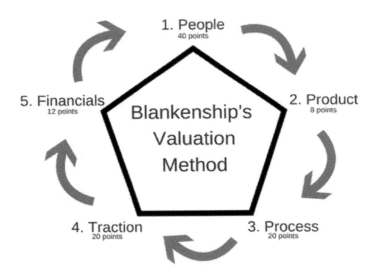

To reiterate the criteria for evaluating the "People" section, there were seven questions that added up to a maximum 40 points. These critical questions are:

1. Are the founders of the startup fully committed and working on it full-time? (15 pts.)
2. Do the founding members look like the best possible combo? (15 pts.)

3. How many of the original founders stayed to continue working on the startup? (2 pts.)
4. Do any of the founders have the potential to become icons that can stand out to the public? (2 pts.)
5. Are the founders experienced in managing their finances? (2 pts.)
6. Would you trust the founders with a blank check upon conducting a credit and background check? (2 pts.)
7. Are the founders responsive to your ideas? (2 pts.)

Remember that the people are the most important factor in guaranteeing a successful investment. You are investing in the people who operate and believe in the company. Make sure that the founder embodies all of the characteristics of the PACED acronym (Passionate, Ambivert, Calculated Risk Taker, Erudite, and Dedicated).

Check to see if the three key roles (Hacker, Hustler, and Growth Hacker) are present in the founding team. If the startup you are thinking about investing in does not have all of these elements, it will be a better idea to spend your investment dollars elsewhere.

3

Product
Make Customers Love What You've Built

"The aim of marketing is to know and understand the customer so well that the product or service fits him and sells itself"
-Peter Drucker

Despite the most important aspect in the Blankenship Valuation Method being to search for brilliantly-driven founders, it is also important to evaluate the quality of the startup's product. A well-made product that creates habits and dependencies is the difference between a sustainable and forgettable brand. The Blankenship Valuation Method helps determine whether or not a product is the right investment for you by calculating financial risk versus possible reward.

The Blankenship Valuation Method should help you form the right decisions through objective measurements, not subjective "gut feelings" and primarily intuition. If you're investing in a startup because of its product, you still need to use the reason and science rooted in the Blankenship Valuation Method.

The Blankenship Valuation Method awards 8 possible points to the "Product" section. The 8 points are broken down into 8 different but related questions. Prospective investors should ask themselves:

1. Do you enjoy the product enough that you really want to invest in it? (1 pt.)
2. Is the total addressable market ("TAM") large enough to care about? (1 pt.)
3. Is there verifiable demand for the product? (2 pts.)
4. Are people addicted to and obsessed with the product? (0.5 pt.)
5. Does the product experience significant repeat business? (1 pt.)
6. Is the product likely going to be around for at least 20 years? (0.5 pt.)
7. Is the average net increase in revenue linear, impressive, and sustainable? (1 pt.)
8. Is the product massively and openly shared? (1 pt.)

Enjoy the Product

The most important rule when investing is being able to believe in the product. The easiest way to believe in a product is through trying and enjoying it. If you do not enjoy the product, customers won't either. Although people have different preferences, i.e. wants and needs, I suggest that you refrain from investing your time and money in products that you don't absolutely love. You will not be as enthusiastic about investing and will more likely be reluctant to work with the company. If that is the case, it is better to just look for a different startup.

You should not be afraid to use the product, put it through your own tests, and ask any questions that you may have while doing so. The best startups and products will have you excited about everything it offers. It is wiser to invest in products where you personally feel joy and the potential for amazing sales and sustainable, growing revenue.

Total Addressable Market

The Total Addressable Market (TAM) relates to the revenue opportunity that is available for profit. It may be difficult to determine the TAM, but you should make educated guesses before investing. Ideally, the market's potential should be at least $20 billion dollars or more, and you should hope that the startup is able to achieve 5% market share within 24 months. And long-term, it is ideal that the startup is able to reach a complete monopoly.

A good question to ask is whether or not the product has the ability to create a completely new market. For example, Apple created its own market via the iTunes ecosystem by tapping into the older audio market of CDs, cassette tapes, and records. I would recommend reading Peter Thiel's "Zero to

One" to receive an understanding of how to create markets that are currently nonexistent. The book also discusses how products should be original and not a clone in order to improve the chance of monopolization. Although Google is not the only search engine, it is by far the most dominant. It is a good idea to ask yourself if the product you would like to invest in is original and has a respectable chance of becoming a monopoly.

Verifiable Demand

In "The Lean Startup", author Eric Ries encourages startups to develop a Minimum Viable Product (MVP). A MVP is a functioning demo of the product and its key features. As an investor, it is best to avoid companies that do not have a demo available to test. The demo should be usable in order to prove demand and simple enough for people to possibly understand, enjoy and mention it to others.

Verifiable demand is just as important as having the Minimum Viable Product. You should clearly recognize the product's demand before you invest because a product without demand will not sell and be profitable. The demand should be high, and growth should be linear or exponential, preferably between 5% and 10% monthly. If a company

Ross' Lesson: investors need to determine whether or not there's demand beyond the growth charts one finds on an average startup's pitch deck.

struggles to understand statistical data relevant to the growth of its website and product, it is difficult to verify whether or not true demand exists. Google Analytics is a helpful tool to check a company's online presence through its website's statistics. Another valuable verification method is by directly speaking with customers and asking for honest feedback. You could also ask someone trustworthy to use the product and give his or her opinion.

Next, you will want to verify a company's tax returns. You are looking for gross revenue and the amount of tax being paid. Those are the most accurate numbers in allowing you to sense whether or not a company is indeed as successful as it claims to be.

However, you are not finished after these steps. You should visit the company's office to see how people interact with customers. You should assess whether or not the employees are genuinely excited to assist them or if they perceive customers as chores. This applies more to retail startups and may not be possible with all companies. For example, a company that provides an online service would not be a good candidate for this.

Do not get involved with a product that has not been created yet due to insufficient funds and a product too complicated to explain to others. If it costs too much to make a demo, it is not the right product for your investment dollars. It is better to spend your money on proven products with real potential. That is not to say that products like those have never worked out, but it is a long shot that you would be safer avoiding. You will be prouder and more secure about the investment portfolio that you are building.

Addicted to Product, Repeat Business, and 20-Year Life Time Value

A product needs to have at least one noteworthy special quality, or "X-Factor," that makes it unique and better than the products that are already on the market. An effective X-Factor raises the probability of customers repeatedly using and becoming addicted to the product. An addicted custo base increases brand loyalty, brand awareness, and custome lifetime value (CLV).

There are several benefits in getting people addicted to your product. People who are addicted to a product are more likely to continue using it even without company intervention. For example, fanatics of Apple will eagerly wait for and purchase the latest devices, and hooked Facebook users will continually update their profiles, statuses, and pictures. These customers eventually become evangelists of the product, sharing it with their peers and providing free endorsement for the company. It is much easier for customers to introduce a product to others that has both beneficial and addictive features. Uber users can conveniently offer personalized discount codes, and Facebook users can share articles, pictures, and videos on the platform. By creating addictive products and devising marketing strategies that generate repeat business, companies will extend the reach of their brand, for the long-term.

Ross' Lesson: one of the most important things on the path to profitability is repeat-business and an extended lifetime value of a startup's customer.

Addiction extends beyond simply being enamored by a single product. It establishes brand loyalty. Addicted customers who are loyal to a brand will cause repeat business, not just for the initial product but also for others that the company created. For example, Adobe utilizes a Software as a Service (SaaS) model and offers a variety of products, which make it convenient for consumers to purchase multiple programs because they are in one place. An addictive product with a solid base of repeat customers can usually be relevant for at least 10 to 20 years. Conversely, products that have a difficult

andwagon effect do not last very long.
nies have to capitalize on transitioning the
repeatedly use one product into lifetime
overall brand.

...p... will increase the customer lifetime value. The companies that are successful and experience longevity have products that cultivate lifetime customers. You want the customer lifetime value to increase, and the cost of customer acquisition to either remain the same or decrease. Growth in the CLV is extremely valuable to the company. When a customer returns monthly or annually and buys a company's products, brand loyalty is developed. The strengthened loyalty and ensuing greater profit margins are what make companies sustainable and able to last for at least 10 to 20 years.

It may be difficult to speculate whether or not a product will be around 20 years from now. However, there are certain questions that can help assess this better. Is there an existing market with competitors, and have they been around for years? If so, how have those products performed on the market? Can the startup's founders monopolize the industry with their product? Can the product's name be transformed into a verb (e.g. "Google or Uber it")? If the answer to the majority of these questions is yes, there is a much higher chance that the product to still be around in 20 years.

Serious investors know that the way to build wealth is through investing in companies that carry products with lasting operational capabilities. There are many products that are trendy and sell insanely well, but disappear after such temporary hype. For example, MySpace was more popular than Facebook for about three years before MySpace collapsed. Facebook's registration philosophy of using real names and identities was more appealing to the general public than MySpace's, which allowed profiles to be created using anonymous and fake names. Although some people may see those products as an opportunity to make a quick buck, you should avoid them. In order to reliably build lifetime wealth and security, you should account for long-term potential and invest your money in companies that will most likely be around for decades. Upon doing so, you will have the means to get involved with even more startups in the future.

Apple

The importance of a company's people and its product cannot be overstated. A fantastic example of that is Apple. When Steve Jobs pitched his first personal computer in 1976, investors liked Jobs' abilities and believed in the quality of his product. Although Apple started with a simple idea, it successively introduced new products that became popular, growing its brand and boasting a market capitalization worth hundreds of billions of dollars. It is now an iconic brand that is recognized by nearly everyone. It has gotten to the point where it may even be safe to say that you are in the minority if you do not own an Apple product.

Apple has a brand culture that extends well beyond just marketing. Apple receives new customers and repeat business more than its competitors because of its dedicated evangelists and fan base. The people follow the company's news almost religiously and share any announcements with their peers. Therefore, the products that Apple offers annually are always met with great attention. For a lot of those people, they will not be satisfied with anything less than an Apple product, and even the slightest thought of purchasing from another company does not cross their minds. Having an Apple product to them symbolizes having an innovative and design-driven technology. As I stated in my last book, "Apple continually positions itself as a bastion of innovation, design, and imagination, and that comes across in the consumer culture." (Blankenship, Kings Over Aces p. 75)

Uber

Another valuable company that provides a good example is Uber. Uber began in San Francisco around July of 2010, and in just a few years, it has developed, grown, and taken over the transportation market, valuing over $50 billion dollars. Uber cars have practically replaced taxis. Whenever you need a ride, you can use the Uber app on your phone to request a driver who will usually appear within minutes to take you wherever you need to go. Now, it offers food delivery as well. Since Uber partnered with McDonalds, you can even get a Big Mac and fries delivered to your doorstep in most communities. Uber is revolutionizing the already existing transportation and food delivery industries and making them better.

If you tried Uber when it first began, you would have probably thought that it was a fresh, interesting, and convenient way to get around town. Although Uber served the same purpose as taxis, the slightly different and enjoyable vibe was enough to give it a strong customer base, staying power, and value to investors. As I mentioned in my book, "No new problems or overall solutions may exist, but new approaches do. We look for founders with creative, intelligent, and marketable approaches. Travis Kalanick's approach with Uber was to convert a growing reliance on crowdsource models in technical and Internet fields to a new field: transportation." (Blankenship, Kings Over Aces p. 51) Prospective investors must see whether or not a product has the potential to be around for decades. Upon gaining popularity, "Ubering" became a verb generally understood by the public. Similar to "Googling it", people have replaced the phrase, "Let's grab a cab" with "Let's Uber." That is a great sign for Uber and its goals for longevity.

However, Uber has faced its fair share of adversities. It is the largest company still in startup mode, and despite a $60 billion dollar valuation, it has not yet been profitable. Clones of Uber, such as Lyft, have also made their way onto the scene and increased competition. The increase in competition has forced Uber to lower its ride fares, resulting in a loss of net revenue. Uber also dealt with the repercussions of not appointing the right leaders and staff. It has undergone a change in leadership with Travis Kalanick, the CEO and founder, being replaced by Dara Khosrowshahi due to legal issues regarding ethical breaches. Although it was the mid-level managers and not Kalanick who caused those problems, it demonstrated the importance of hiring competent and respectful staff.

Uber has a multi-billion-dollar product but needs the correct leadership to guide and continue its success. Khosrowshahi has attempted to improve Uber's damaged reputation by hiring better employees with the same long-term vision. He also plans to change Uber's image to be more driver-friendly than predatory. However, only time will tell if Uber is indeed headed back in the right direction.

Buffer and inDinero

Although nearly everyone has heard about Apple and Uber, people may not have heard about Buffer or inDinero. I was an early-stage investor in both companies and believe that they will eventually become billion-dollar enterprises. The reason is because they offer valuable products and services that help other businesses operate better, which is extremely conducive to success. Those are the types of companies that you should look to invest in too.

Buffer is a platform for any business, individual, or marketer that want to automate the posts that they put on their social media websites. It implements a SaaS subscription model and sees millions of dollars in revenue growth. Users find it addictive, fun, and helpful when they set up their social media in this manner. People who do not use Buffer will probably not experience as much marketing success and may want to consider trying it.

inDinero is a more innovative way than QuickBooks for combining products and services and tracking incoming revenue and expenses. It should help you make better financial decisions for your business. You can see exactly which areas require attention when you are aiming to cut costs or increase growth. Business leaders recognize how valuable such a product is in raising the quality of their businesses.

Both Buffer and inDinero serve as great examples of businesses with products that are liked and needed. Everyone aims to reduce expenses, increase revenue, and be profitable. A successful product should have the qualities of enjoyment and necessity. Just like how I tried both products before investing in them, you should also make sure that you test drive every product in which you're considering an investment.

Linear vs. Exponential Growth

When you are assessing growth, first pay attention to the market. Growth cannot continue if the market for the product will eventually saturate and the need to purchase it will disappear. People have to be able to continually buy the product out of a feeling of necessity. They should feel like replacing the product once it wears out and acquiring it if they do not already own one.

Meaningful and linear growth is better than growth metrics that are uncontrollable and insane to maintain. There are a couple of questions that can help better picture the amount of revenue earned. What is the product's average monthly growth? How many free and paid unique users are there each month? That information has to be provided through verifiable data. The next suggestion is more applicable to SaaS (subscription model-based) startups. In order to understand how much revenue is exactly generated, you want to look at the monthly recurring revenue (MRR) and compare how much a company makes month-to-month. For example, if you visit buffer.baremetrics.com you'll see their monthly recurring revenue and how much growth they have each month. The statistics should show stable growth.

In the first year of a business's operation, the growth of its product should ideally be exponential. However, it is more important for the business to experience sustainable, strong, and linear growth during the first two years, ranging between 5% and 10% monthly. After two years, you can normalize the growth and perceive the product as sustainable. If those conditions are met, then you should determine whether or not the company is worthy of your investment.

You want companies to be open and transparent with their data. It is an excellent way to understand what they do and how well they do it. For example, the company Buffer discloses its monthly growth and MRR at buffer.baremetrics.com. You should still be wary of the charts that companies provide because they may be biased and misleading to make the companies' results look more favorable. Therefore, it is important to pick and choose the right and relevant information to evaluate. Another alternative is to use third-party data sources such as Google Analytics.

Massively and Openly Shared

Open sharing is a recent phenomenon and commonly employed strategy among businesses. Companies have figured out that they may lose a significant amount of revenue by placing parameters that prevent people from sharing their products. Although restrictions may stop non-paying customers from using a product, it has also shown that people turn away from such products and seek other alternatives. Netflix serves as a good example of how companies can benefit from allowing open sharing. People are able to share accounts with each other and appreciate being able to do that. If Netflix did not allow people to share accounts, there would most likely be fewer users. Open sharing may be implemented in the pre-revenue stage (e.g. Facebook) or the post-revenue stage (Apple). Students were talking about Facebook even before it became available in their colleges. I wanted to see what the hype was about with Facebook and was able to use a friend's account while he was attending Harvard. Both Netflix and Facebook show that open sharing can effectively build excitement when used correctly.

Expanding upon the principles of open sharing and sourcing, I would also suggest staying away from what I call, "stealth startups." Stealth startups are companies that try to fly under the radar and get everything completed before entering the scene. Although that may sound good in theory because it prevents others from possibly seeing and stealing the idea, the company loses the invaluable opportunity of developing a following before the product is released. Garnering interest before the product even comes out helps ensure that it will sell well starting from the beginning. The product will gain momentum, and sales will be above expectations, creating the growth that companies seek.

Buffer exhibits an open sourcing mentality
tries to be open and honest with its plans. It
displaying the different ideas that it is workir
there is the possibility of other companies an
its ideas or leaking information, Buffer is not
that. It understands that openly sharing that type of
information help its followers anticipate whatever comes out
next. The excitement creates loyalty and a repeat customer
base that returns and repeatedly purchases the product.
Buffer demonstrates exactly why it is better to invest in
companies that are transparent and upfront about their
products and business operations.

Get on the Startup Elevator, and Head Up to the Next Level!

When considering a startup's product, it may be helpful to
think about it as an elevator. You should question whether or
not the product has what it takes to get to the next level.
There are several conditions that need to be in place for that
to be possible. I made the **"ELEVATOR"** acronym to
describe those conditions.

Ride Ross' Startup **ELEVATOR** Up. Not Down.

A Product's Levels:

Excitement & enjoyment
Long-lasting brand potential
Evangelical products
Verified Demand and an "MVP"
Average Monthly Growth
Total Addressable Market
Open-sharing
Repeat Business

Ross' Startup Investing **ELEVATOR**.
How far can it climb? IPO? Multibillion Exit?

st, the product needs to generate excitement and joy. The founders of the startup have to enjoy working on it. As an investor, you have to enjoy the product as well. If it is difficult for the founders and investors to find joy in the product, it will most likely also be difficult for the customers. However, brief excitement and happiness is not enough to keep the product sustainable. The product must have the potential to instill those emotions long-term.

Second, the startup should be capable of developing its brand name and recognition over time. The company should be able to become influential enough to transcend colloquialism and have its brand name replace the generally used term. For example, people usually do not ask for a tissue but a Kleenex instead. People do not search. They Google. If the product can achieve a similar feat, it is can evolve into a long-lasting brand.

A great idea and brand helps develop evangelism of a product. Customers will not simply purchase the product but will also become invested in the culture behind it. Since people talk more often about products that they love, they will eagerly discuss it with others and give the company free word-of-mouth advertisement.

If you get involved with the right startup at the right time, you may reap the rewards and build your wealth off of a generational product. Companies such as Apple, Facebook, Uber, Buffer, and inDinero possess brands and cultures that their users can easily evangelize. Those companies and the people who founded and invested in them have felt the value of those qualities. Hopefully, you can invest in the next big startup and experience the benefits of a powerful brand firsthand. Just remember to always use the product before determining whether or not it is worth evangelizing.

Conclusion: A Final Thought on the Product

Upon reading about why a great product is an important factor in having a successful investment, it is now a good time to reiterate the Blankenship Valuation Method's criteria for assessing a high-quality product. Eight points can be awarded to a startups overall score by answering yes or no to eight questions. They are:

1. Do you enjoy the product enough that you really want to invest in it? (1 pt.)
2. Is the total addressable market ("TAM") large enough to care about? (1 pt.)
3. Is there verifiable demand for the product? (2 pts.)
4. Are people addicted to and obsessed with the product? (0.5 pt.)
5. Does the product experience significant repeat business? (1 pt.)
6. Is the product likely going to be around for at least 20 years? (0.5 pt.)
7. Is the average net increase in revenue linear, impressive, and sustainable? (1 pt.)
8. Is the product massively and openly shared? (1 pt.)

The information that followed after the initial introduction of the criteria should have helped answer the eight questions better. The majority of great products should have fared well, earning somewhere between six and eight points. The generational products should have earned seven or eight. Hopefully, the investment you were looking at fared well when tested.

And remember, there are **five main reasons** why startups fail that are related to the product. They are:

1. No demand from the market.
2. Wrong timing, either being too early or too late.

3. Only an app instead of a company with a number of product offerings
4. A clone of a product that does not offer anything unique.
5. Way too complicated and gives people trouble understanding its features.

Next, we will discuss how a startup's plans, roadmaps, and the process it undergoes to accomplish its goals are important for its success.

4

Process
A Winning Aspect of Investment Valuation

"Trust the process."

-Marcus Lemonis

Establishing a Process That Supports Fully Automated Revenue Generation

The next 20 points you can potentially award using the "Blankenship Valuation Method" apply to the process utilized by the startup in question. A full evaluation of the process stage requires that you look at two key areas in the startup's operations.

The first is the internal process utilized in the structure of the company. You should ask, "Who exactly is in charge here?" to determine how company roles are assigned and executed in both the first and second year of operations.

The second area will explore the external process as it pertains to creating a scalable billion-dollar enterprise. In this realm, automation is key. You will look at the external method to determine if a manual process has evolved into a suitably automated system that will scale well in the coming years.

The existence of these two factors – clear roles and automation - helps ensure the startup has a foundation that will facilitate the traction phase for sustainable growth. Since a great process drives better traction, this valuation phase remains the second most important aspect of the Blankenship Valuation Method.

Binary Evaluation Makes Point Assignment Simple

The point allocation for this phase is a binary "yes" or "no" assignment that will give the startup a maximum of 20 points. Each ten-point allocation can only be assigned if the startup meets all aspects of each rule. Otherwise, the startup will receive zero points for that area and will need to work on fulfilling those requirements to move forward in raising investment capital.

Since startups must exceed 90 points for the seed phase, and steadily increase from there, meeting the requirements for these two areas is of utmost importance. Remember to remain completely objective in your evaluations to ensure the startups have what it takes to become the next billion-dollar empire. If the startup does not have clear roles from the beginning and fails to employ an automated process in the second year, then your only option is to give them zero points for both categories.

In my experience, startups without these factors just don't have the operational model required for sustainable growth and true success in their markets. Therefore, only startups with clear roles and plans for automation are in line to receive investment dollars from the seed stage and beyond. Remember, clear startup roles and a seamless delivery system inspire customers to keep buying a company's products.

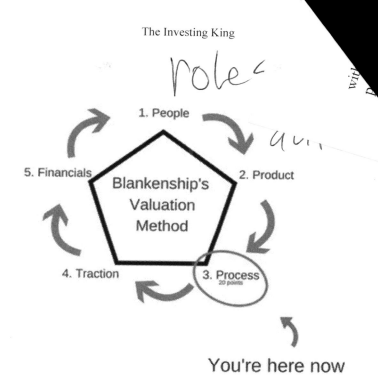

role *av* *w* *with*

You're here now

From Process to Traction: Fulfill the Capture Requirement

The presence of a great process allows the traction phase to have a naturally positive impact on the growth of the startup. Therefore, these two areas are inherently linked in my valuation method. To better display how these two areas interact, I have created the **CAPTURE** acronym with clear definitions for each step.

C̲reate Clear Roles Within the Company Environment (10 points)

The first step looks at whether the startup has established clear Hacker, Hustler and Growth Hacker roles for product development, sales, and customer engagement activities, respectively. When concrete roles are assigned, the startup has the foundation needed for their market success. Startups n clear core roles assigned from day one, earn a binary 10 points, while those with ambiguous role assignments do not receive any points.

Automate the Delivery of the Product (10 points)

To assign the next 10 points, you must look at the startup's ability to automate their product delivery methods by their second year. Although startups tend to complete tasks by hand in their first year, they must have a concrete plan to automate after 12 months of launch. Otherwise, the startup does not have the structure required for sustainable, scalable growth. If automation plans exist, award the points; if not, then zero points should be given for this step.

Produce a Need or Dependency for the Product (5 points)

The third step explores whether the startup's product produces a need or an addictive element. Customers and businesses should find that the product has an evangelical quality that makes it noteworthy and sharable. The product should also provide true value to the client base in its ability to resolve the identified problems, making it a "must-have" element in their lives. Products that produce a need earn the startup five points.

Talk to Customers and Employ Thought Leadership Tactics (5 points)

The founders of the startup must become thought leaders in their industry to achieve billion-dollar success. They must discuss the problems they have identified by talking with their customers and by positioning their product as a surefire way to resolve those difficulties. Startups can employ thought leadership activities on their blogs and social media accounts to create a strong following. If the startup talks with their customers and employs thought leadership tactics, award them five points.

Understand the Needs of Your Customers and Competitors (3 points)

The fifth step builds on the fourth by asking if the startup understands the needs of their customers and competitors. As the interests of their client base evolve, the startup must adapt to support the needs identified in their industry. The founding team must be able to evolve their operations, without pivoting, to fulfill the requirements of this section. If the startup exhibits this quality, give them three points.

Respond to Customer Requests, Complaints and Comments (2 points)

When it comes to supporting their customer base, startups must commit to responding quickly to requests, complaints, and comments. However, a quick response isn't always fulfilling the customer's request, sometimes it is best to say, "No." Saving time and effort by denying unreasonable or unfulfillable requests can be just as powerful in the end, particularly for a startup with limited time. The ability to provide quick responses to their customers earns the startup two points.

Energy Savings: Understand Why They Matter (5 points)

Startups must ask where they can save time and money to best channel their energy. Finding the best sales and customer engagement channels allows the startup to achieve sustainable growth without spending too much time and energy. Utilizing certain cost-effective strategies will allow the product to become profitable quicker without draining the startup of their existing funds or squandering valuable time. For this last step, award five points if the startup employs effective energy-saving practices.

With process revolving around the first two letters, and traction surrounding the rest, this acronym clearly depicts the link between these two aspects of my valuation method. As you move forward with valuation, you can determine if the startup has established the process areas that will lead to great traction along the way.

Team Function Matters: An Exploration of the Internal Process

A well-aligned internal process with clear founder roles will win startups 10 points for the process category. You must identify if the startup established their roles from day one, and remains focused on their assigned tasks. Even with clear roles, founders must remain willing to fulfill their roles and delegate as needed for the success of the company.

Knowing who is in charge of each aspect of the internal process will allow you to see if the company has the structure required for market success. Understand every facet of this area to determine if the startup in question deserves to receive the next 10 points in my valuation method. The next section will review the three main roles that all winning startups should have starting from day one.

What Roles Should the Founding Team Fill?

Billion-dollar startups always have three main roles fulfilled from day one: the Hacker, the Hustler, and the Growth Hacker. Let's review how these roles are defined to see if you can identify these individuals in the

Ross' Lesson: startups should never outsource any of these three key roles. Outsourcing involves hiring people that are loosely connected to the startup but are not part of the core team.

founding team of the startups you evaluate.

Hacker

The Hacker devotes time to developing the minimum viable product, or MVP, from the ground up. In many startup companies, the Hacker goes by the official designation of Chief Technology Officer (CTO).

Hackers tend to have a background in programming or product development that allows them to personally create the MVP, in-house. The Hacker must be able to produce the MVP in 30 days without relying on outsourcing in any way. At the bare minimum, the Hacker should be able to create a landing page for the startup to present at meetings with potential investors.

Hustler

The Hustler focuses on drumming up interest in the product through direct interaction with customers by using inbound marketing techniques. The Hustler may also have the title of Chief Financial Officer (CFO), President of Sales or business developer while fulfilling this role.

An effective Hustler has immense charisma, a friendly demeanor and an affable approach to excel as the startup's sales leader. In fact, the startup's Hustler must be able to sell the product before it is even developed to verify need and demand for that entity. Ambiverts, a balance between introverts and extroverts, tend to excel in this role due to their ability to talk and listen in turn to engage with customers.

Growth Hacker

Growth Hackers utilize social media and marketing platforms to engage with current and potential customers. Since

Growth Hackers tend to expertly harness the power of social media platforms, this role may be called "Social Media Maven," though Public Relations (PR) and Human Resources (HR) designations are often utilized as well.

An effective Growth Hacker creates a narrative for the startup and makes sure the product is growing through every phase of development. The Growth Hacker's approach may include the production of engaging SEO content that speaks to the problems of the industry and the solutions afforded by their product.

Knowing these three roles will help you determine if a startup will experience sustainable growth in the future. Many other roles may become a part of the startup's structure, but these three roles must exist from the very first day. Without these roles, the startup can neither produce a winning MVP nor achieve any growth.

Can the CEO Fulfill All Three Roles in the First Year?

Even with these three roles in place, the CEO of the startup must also be able to act as the Hacker, Hustler and Growth Hacker as needed. By fulfilling these roles, the CEO will better understand the strengths and weaknesses of the startup. As a result, the CEO will also be able to make better decisions for the company's future.

Ross' Lesson: CEO's must be ready, willing, and able to take on any role at the drop of a dime.

Roles Will Change – and That's Okay

After the startup has been in operation for one year, the roles may change as the company environment responds to the needs of their customer base in the second year. You may notice that the roles take on a nebulous appearance and titles become permeable along the way, and that's okay.

As the roles adjust, make sure to verify that the delegation of duties continues to follow the Hacker, Hustler and Growth Hacker structure. The specialists in these categories, and the positions established through company growth must remain focused on their job duties. When the founding team and its employees stay focused and have established roles, the company can forge ahead like a racehorse to the finish line.

When Teams Have Clear Roles, Everybody Wins

Studying the structure of today's billion-dollar companies at their earliest stages will help you understand the importance of the establishment of clear roles from day one.

Facebook

The social media platform, Facebook, started its journey toward its multi-billion-dollar valuation as a small startup consisting of four key individuals. Mark Zuckerberg and Dustin Moskovitz acted as the Hackers for the current iteration of Facebook by establishing its main platform, which began as TheFacebook.com. These two Hackers had toyed around with a similar concept, Facemash, before forging ahead with their billion-dollar idea.

To fulfill the Hustler and Growth Hacker roles, Zuckerberg brought in two classmates, Eduardo Saverin and Chris Hughes. Saverin acted as the business manager to help Facebook acquire its first advertisers, while Hughes increased engagement by interacting with the customers and press. With these roles fulfilled by dedicated individuals, the founding team could focus on complete domination of the marketplace and earn billions of dollars in revenue.

Unicorn status indicates startups that have the potential to achieve their billion-dollar dreams in the near future. However, at Angel Kings, we look for unicorns with real wings that can fly. Unicorns with wings are companies that are looking to achieve early profitability along with high growth. As mentioned earlier, two companies I have had the pleasure of identifying and investing in as unicorns with real wings are Buffer and inDinero. Their founders' ability to establish and follow clear roles in the startup structure helped make these two companies winning investments in my venture capital portfolio.

Ross' Lesson: investors should be looking for more than the hype (unicorn) and rather for profitability (unicorns with real wings).

Buffer

Innovator Joel Gascoigne set out to bring Buffer to life using a lean startup approach. To support this approach, Joel worked with Co-founder and Chief Operating Officer, Leo Widrich, as the Hacker, Hustler and Growth Hacker. The two of them filled all the necessary roles needed for a successful startup in Buffer's beginning stages.

Joel first identified the need for an app that could allow marketers to schedule social media posts and automate their marketing activities. Thus, he created a landing page to see if enough people were interested in the product to make it a profitable venture. After verifying the demand for the initial MVP, Joel set out in the creation of that platform all while acting as a thought leader in this realm through his dedicated blog. As a Growth Hacker, he regularly completed interviews with the press and directly interacted with his customer base. The result was a platform that could stand on its own and grow sustainably well into the future.

inDinero

The founders of inDinero, Jessica Mah and Andy Su, teamed up to create and market a platform that would resolve the need for excellent financial tools for small businesses. Jessica acted as both the Hustler and Growth Hacker to tell the world about their platform and keep customers engaged with its features. Andy acted as the Hacker by designing the platform and establishing updates as needed for its complete success. Their ability to assign and follow these clear roles from the beginning allowed them to focus on fulfilling the needs of the small business owners who made up their client base.

The establishment of clear roles within the startup's structure not only benefits the founding team but their investors as well. As an investor, when you see startups with these three roles fulfilled, you can forge ahead with the valuation process, knowing you have a winning team on the books. This allows you to confidently move through my valuation method without wasting time on startups that just do not have what it takes to succeed.

Both Buffer and inDinero exemplify the perfect process of how startups should begin. Not only do they have two top founders who fill every role as needed, but they also clearly delegated who's doing what from day one.

Were You Able to Award the 10 Points for This Section?

To determine if the startup is like Buffer or inDinero, and will receive 10 points for the creation of clear roles, use the three following questions to make this determination:

ere someone creating the MVP in-house without
ıeed for any outsourcing?

:s someone meet with customers and sell the
duct, even before it is developed?

3. Is there someone available to engage with customers
and keep interest levels up?

If you can answer a resounding "Yes," to *all three questions*,
give the startup 10 points. Just one or two "Yes," answers will
not do in this binary evaluation. If all three roles are not
established, assign zero points to this category.

Remember to Identify Potential **BUILD** Issues

My **BUILD** acronym was developed to help you identify and
remember the potential problems facing startups as they build
their founding team and expand with hiring new employees.

Building in a Vacuum

When startups build in a vacuum, they eliminate their ability
to improve their products and processes in meaningful ways.
Startups must open up their operations and communicate
with customers directly to create products and processes that
help them achieve positive, sustainable growth.

Unwillingness to Take on Other Tasks

With the help of employees, startup founders must be willing
to take on other tasks to keep the company operations
moving forward with purpose. If you see any unwillingness of
a startup founder to take on other roles, that's a red flag.
Founders must always be willing to assume roles as needed.

Inability to Delegate as Needed

Although taking on alternative tasks is important when necessary, knowing when to delegate also plays a role in the potential success of a startup. Startup founders must break away from the urge to micromanage and openly delegate responsibilities to remain focused on their own assigned tasks.

Little is Completed In-House

Startups should always build in-house first and rely on an inside sales team to get the job done. Outsourcing key tasks such as product development and sales makes it impossible for the founder to improve their product and processes.

Don't Know Who's in Charge

When no one knows who is in charge, it's like a rudderless ship without direction. Identifying who is in charge of each role, and the startup in general can keep the founders moving toward their goal of becoming the next billion-dollar empire.

Touch on each of these points to see if the startup in question has the elements that help predict success in the marketplace. If the startup has any of the problems mentioned in my **BUILD** acronym, then it will likely have problems further down the road and is not the best choice for your investment capital.

Become Automated Within Twelve Months

Successful startups should fully automate their operations after the first year. Before the automation phase, startups can perform their product creation and support tasks by hand without worry, as long as a plan for future automation is in place. An examination of the startup's plan for complete automation will allow you to award an additional 10 points using the Blankenship Valuation Method.

Can the Startup Make Money While Sleeping?

Founders should try to make money while they are sleeping. In order to make money while sleeping, a startup needs to upgrade their platform to become fully automated. This means removing the tedious tasks, such as constant one-to-one user interactions and manual on-boarding, and having your platform do it for you. Startups should plan on removing redundancies and create automated efficiencies, from day one.

Second Year Plans: Automation on the Horizon

Startups are nearly always built manually in their earliest stages. If the startup founders continue doing everything by hand, without plans for automation, their operations cannot scale into a billion-dollar empire. Therefore, by the second year, startup founders must enact their plans for automation to begin creating their scalable enterprise. To ensure automation happens by this key period, founders must have their plans in the works several months before this point.

How Automation Builds Billion-Dollar Empires

Time and time again, startup case studies prove that automation builds billion-dollar empires. Airbnb is the most intriguing of the startups that has moved from a hands-on process to full automation - and achieved success as a result. Facebook is another example that started as a manually populated platform and ended up fully automated through word of mouth signups.

Airbnb

The founders of Airbnb created their startup in 2008 to empower homeowners to rent out their available spaces and make more money. Their company started as "Air Bed N Breakfast" to give people options beyond the typical hotel room, especially when these customers faced a lack of suitable lodging options in their area. The hotel and lodging industry had never experienced such a revolutionary way of operating before Airbnb hit the market.

The founders started by looking on Craigslist for listings that featured rooms and homes available for short-term rentals. Upon finding these listings, the founders would email those individuals, one by one, and invite them to list their properties on their new platform. Manual growth hacking at its finest allowed this startup to achieve recognition and followers, but it did not allow for sustainable, scalable growth.

To support their continued growth, the founders joined Y-Combinator, a popular startup incubator, and set about making their MVP to automate the core functionality of their product. They also changed their name to a much more marketable brand name, "Airbnb." The platform exploded in popularity as users were able to easily list their rentals on the platform and market their listings online as well. Due to the automating the process, this company has grown into an empire worth more than $30 billion dollars today.

Facebook

At a glance, Facebook seems like it has always been automated, but that was not the case. Zuckerberg had to hand populate the initial users by hacking into the Harvard directory and housing database to acquire the information he needed to contact students directly. He wrote emails to each student directly inviting them to join the site and interact with their peers in his new online environment. Even with the use of a manual process, Zuckerberg's site grew to have thousands of users in less than 48 hours.

As interest in the site grew, he began working toward the creation of a fully automated signup process using a PHP-based development tool. As users joined this new social media platform, they organically invited their friends and family onboard, which grew Facebook into the massive entity it is today. This social media empire boasts a multi-billion-dollar valuation and continues to grow in popularity year after year.

These two case studies prove that the sky is the limit when it comes to market success through automation. Without automation, both of these companies would have experienced limited growth based on the founders' ability to perform the required tasks by hand.

How to Apply 10 Points for This Section?

As a binary measure, the 10 points available for this section relies on the presence of a surefire plan to automate by the second year. If the startup in question does not plan to automate or has not made any progress in establishing a realistic plan, they should not receive 10 points.

Remember not to judge the startup for completing their tasks by hand in the first year, as every successful empire begins in this way. A startup that completes every last initial task by hand can easily automate if they have a solid plan in place. Ask the startup about plans for automation and base your point allocation on that factor alone.

As you look at the startup's plan to automate, ask key questions that reveal if their intended actions align with their company goals and operations. If you determine that the plans to automate are realistic and obtainable, award 10 points to the startup.

An Excellent Process Paves the Way to Better Traction

When an excellent process surrounds the company operations, the startup can achieve real traction in driving customers to the product. A great product cannot sell itself, and startups fail every day due to placing all their bets on their MVP selling itself.

The team must position themselves behind the product to help it gain the interest and support of their customer base. With each startup founder completing the tasks associated with their concrete roles, the product can dominate the marketplace and gain an evangelical following.

Moving forward with automation allows founders to refocus their efforts on pursuing sustainable growth for their startup through new customer acquisitions and additional product development. Automation allows founders to make money while they complete other tasks - and while they sleep. With time, the startup can achieve sustainable growth and reach great heights that would have been impossible without the establishment of core roles and full automation.

Startups that embody these characteristics, and earn all 20 points for this section of the Blankenship Valuation Process, have the basic structure needed to become the next billion-dollar companies in their industry. Of course, the rest of the valuation numbers must fall in line before you invest in the company.

The best part about creating solid internal and external processes is the startup's ability to naturally attract customers to their product. The internal process arrangement gives the startup a foundation that will continue supporting their growth well into the future. The startup can add specialty roles to their company's structure to fulfill the evolving needs of their customers without impacting the core roles fulfilled by the founders.

Furthermore, the transformation from a hands-on startup to a fully automated company allows the founders to direct their attention to growth. The automated process opens up doors for sustainable growth that would not be achievable while performing every last task by hand.

In the next chapter, you will learn about the remainder of the **CAPTURE** acronym to explore how traction helps startups grow into billion-dollar enterprises. As you study this facet of the acronym, remember how the creation of clear roles and automation of the product contribute to better traction along the way.

5

Traction
The Driving Force Behind a Successful Startup

"Right now, there's way too much hype on the technologies and not enough attention to the real businesses behind them."
-Mark Cuban

An excellent founding team, winning process, and phenomenal product create a great foundation for a startup's success, but, it doesn't end there. The startup must also commit to establishing traction that drives customers to their product and creates a strong following for the brand.

The traction section of the Blankenship Valuation Method builds on the **CAPTURE** acronym introduced in the last chapter.

Here are the essential steps you need to know:

<u>C</u>reate clear roles for the founding team.
<u>A</u>utomate product delivery within 12 months.
<u>P</u>roduce a need for the product or "MVP."
<u>T</u>alk openly with the community, customers, and competitors.
<u>U</u>nderstand your customers' needs and desires.
<u>R</u>espond promptly to all customer correspondences.
<u>E</u>nergy savings need to be a main priority.

While the first two letters – C and A - center around the clear roles of a company and automation of the product within 12 months, the traction section covers the five remaining letters in our helpful acronym. These seven steps are designed to streamline the valuation process, so you can quickly assess each startup's potential to become the next billion-dollar empire.

Before diving into this 20-point section of the Blankenship Valuation Method, it is important to see how traction drives customers to embrace the company and its MVP.

Produce a Need for the Product or "MVP"

The minimum viable product, or MVP, is a good or service that creates an immediate, positive, and repetitive response from the customer or business.

Let's take a look at Buffer's MVP:

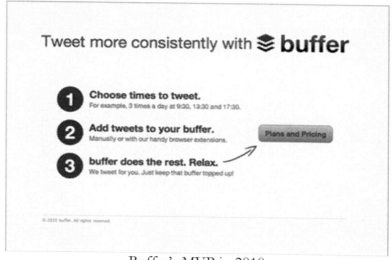

Buffer's MVP in 2010

As you can see, Buffer's MVP was as simple as a landing page with a green button and it only worked for Twitter. Immediately, people understand what Buffer is and how it will positively affect their lives. By setting all your tweets on auto-pilot, Buffer created a way in which marketers could repeat a simple process that allows them to share on social media with ease. But it also saves marketers and employees ample time, and time equals money.

As an investor, you need to make sure that you understand, within the first glance of a startup's MVP, how that MVP will create an immediate, positive, and repetitive success story. Along with a viable MVP, a startup also needs to be obsessed with gaining traction in its earliest days.

Talk Openly with the Community, Customers, and Competitors

Focusing on traction in the early days of the startup will help the startup achieve market share from day one. Transparency is key in establishing a strong following that boosts the startup's potential. If you have to dig for every last bit of information about the startup during the valuation process, you may be right to think that the founders are hiding something. If you see a startup that is not transparent about its product specifications, roadmap, or financial data, be cautious. Doing so prevents customers and investors from engaging with the startup in a meaningful way and it also prevents the investor from obtaining an accurate valuation.

> Ross' Lesson: the most transparent startups are *always* the most successful.

TRANSPARENT

Maintaining an open dialogue about these areas will not open up doors for idea theft from competitors if the startup has a great founding team, streamlined process, and surefire MVP. Customers also respect transparent startups and are more likely to buy from them and become evangelists who tells their friends about the product. In fact, transparency has the power to phenomenally boost traction that allows the startup to grab hold of a large share of the market.

Understand Your Customers' Needs and Desires

When brands utilize memorable marketing tactics to engage their customer base, they allow customers to interact with that company by sharing the content and starting discussions. Effective marketing tactics for startups revolve around meaningful content, emotional displays and useful information that provides value to the consumer. Memorable marketing tactics open the door for a continued relationship with customers viewing that content.

Win Them Over with Actionable Marketing Strategies

Uber is a perfect example of a startup that thinks outside the box to utilize memorable marketing tactics whenever possible. One effective marketing strategy they employed urged customers to use their service to send roses to loved ones on Valentine's Day. Their advertisements utilized touching imagery and content, which in turn made customers excited about using Uber.

In other ads, childhood joy and nostalgia were created with a marketing campaign highlighting Uber's ability to provide on-demand ice cream trucks to small and large-scale events of all kinds. Uber's marketing team proudly displayed their service as a necessity even though we all know it's just a fancier version of a taxi cab company.

Uber's smart marketing practices all revolve around actionable content that inspires new customers to try out the presented product and become an evangelical follower. Uber's marketing is brilliant, and many startups can replicate these strategies in new ways.

Respond Promptly to All Customer Correspondences

Having prompt response times and good customer service will create a positive reputation, which will drive new customers and revenue for your startup. Here's a perfect example of how a company responds promptly and courteously to customer's problem or issues:

Energy Savings Need to be a Main Priority

Startups should be focusing all their time and energy into building an MVP and acquiring their first customers. If they are spending any money on attending conferences or useless happy hours, you should avoid these startups. As a rule of thumb, you want to invest in startups that are obsessively innovative, but always nonchalant about attending the next big events and conferences.

A Strong Brand Culture Establishes a Lifelong Following

Communities of evangelical followers tend to develop around the brand culture established by successful companies. When a strong brand culture exists, customers will flock to that product and its brand. When their identity intertwines with the brand culture of a startup, the customer becomes an evangelical follower and may even inspire their community to try out that "must-have" product.

Apple Creates an Iconic Brand Culture

As a tech leader, Apple inspires their customers to break out from the norm and embrace the sheer efficiency of their products. They position their products as hip, state-of-the-art devices that blow the competition out of the water. Their customers identify with their brand by seeing a reflection of themselves in their silhouette-based ads showcasing the newest products. As a result, many consumers find themselves driven to purchase the next iterations of the products.

Asking the Questions that Matter for Traction Valuation

When it comes to the Blankenship Valuation Method traction section, you will have the ability to award up to 20 points. The points are given on a binary basis as you answer, "Yes" or "No" to all the questions for the last five steps of the CAPTURE acronym.

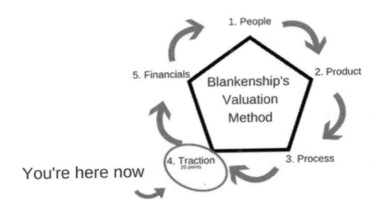

Does the Product Have a Must-Have Quality?

The first five points are awarded if the startup's product creates a "must-have" demand with customers. When it comes to identifying whether there's a need in customers for the startup's product, remember **three rules** for this valuation process.

1. You will be able to determine a clear need within the first 12 months of the startup's operations. If no need exists at that point, the startup has failed to meet this metric.
2. The product must exist for customers to try out and provide feedback on its features and ability to rectify the problems.
3. The product should have an addictive quality that makes customers feel like they cannot live without it. When a product physically exists and attracts an evangelical following within 12 months, the startup may have a winning MVP on their hands.

Four Categories *to Determine Real Need & Dependency*

As startups attempt to fulfill the requirements of this valuation category, they may create demand for their product in **one of four** ways:

1. Social Dependency

Successful products can create demand through social dependency which at its core is about people connecting with others through the startup's product. Facebook and Snapchat, for example, both create a dependency on their products by allowing users to connect with their social networks. Users also gain acceptance within their social circles through the usage of likes and comments. These features help the product stay relevant because people are interested in updating their profiles in attempts to gain more friends, likes, and followers.

2. Convenience Factor

When it comes to product development in this overscheduled world, convenience is king. Startups that can make an activity more convenient and accessible immediately create a need for their product. As you may well know, Uber took the transportation world by storm by allowing their customers to source a ride quickly. As a faster alternative to taxis, Uber allows you to gain access to transportation immediately through a mobile app. The speed and convenience of Uber has replaced taxis completely.

3. Business Empowerment

The ability to empower business owners to purposefully complete their daily operations allows startups' MVPs to gain a natural following in a short period of time. Business owners need the support from purpose-built products to juggle the daily demands of their industry-specific operations. Buffer and inDinero empower business owners by streamlining the marketing and financial-oversight processes, respectively. Both companies provide platforms that allow businesses to manage their workflow easier.

4. Customer Support

Customers need support and empowerment in their own lives too, which opens the doors for startups to fulfill that need with their products. Amazon allows customers to conveniently shop online for almost anything, from anywhere, at any time. Jeff Bezos, Founder and CEO of Amazon, once said, "if you do build a great experience, customers tell each other about that. Word of mouth is very powerful." Before Amazon, finding the lowest prices and acquiring elusive products was not always possible for customers.

Creating Need in a Market Without Existing Demand

The most innovative products don't necessarily need high demand from the start. In fact, startups don't need to scrap their efforts and try something else if they can't identify an immediate demand for their product. When customers enjoy a product enough to tell others, the MVP creates demand by itself to help the startup.

As customers integrate that product into their daily lives, the creation of evangelical followers and word of mouth advertising naturally follows. Of course, startups must create demand within 12 months, or the product will simply fail to create a dependency in its user base.

If you can verify that the product has a clear need in its industry, award the startup five points. If not, don't invest in that startup; you can always restart the valuation process once the startup creates a dependency on its product.

Is the Startup a Thought Leader in Their Industry?

Thought leaders are knowledgeable and trusted sources that give their opinions in their field of expertise in an attempt to educate and inspire others. Thought leadership establishes the startup founders as experts in their industry while creating connections with their customer base. Startups that can act as thought leaders earn five points. The thought leadership process revolves around writing, broadcasting and sharing content that supports the company's narrative.

Content Creation and Distribution

In every field, effective thought leaders create engaging content, share it with their community and interact with their followers through social media, blogs, and other direct channels. These individuals should aim to write at least 500 words a day about topics that concern their industry and their company.

The most successful thought leaders cast a wide net when sharing their content by utilizing multiple channels and automating the process with service providers, like Buffer. When using Buffer, startups can add their thought leadership content to a lineup that will automatically post throughout the year. This hands-off approach to content distribution helps pave the way for customers to see the startup founders as experts in their field.

Press Opportunities

To go one step further, startup founders should always jump at the chance to take advantage of free press opportunities. How? By collaborating with journalists who regularly cover topics in their industry. This collaboration allows startup founders to showcase their skills and expertise while positioning their MVP as a solution to common problems experienced by their customers.

Ross' Lesson: great founders never wait to be noticed. They pave the way for their own success by creating thought leadership within his or her respective industry. This thought leadership is critical long-term to building your brand's reputation and good will.

With press naturally following conventions and other collaborative activities, it makes sense for startup founders to play an important role in the creation of these events. Instead of simply attending the events and getting lost in the crowd, startups can get their name out there by helping organize and hosting conferences, themselves.

Controversy

Controversy gets people talking – and when people are talking about a startup and its products, their interest level heightens as they want to know more about what the company is selling. Therefore, startups should never try to remain safe by taking a neutral stance on tough issues and topics. Instead, they should pick a stance on either side of the discussion and defend their position to give journalists and followers something to talk about to help the company gain publicity.

When Founders Become Thought Leaders, Magic Happens

The conversations inspired by thought leader posts have the potential to open the doors for ongoing dialogue between founders and their customer base.

1. The innovative leader behind Buffer, Joel Gascoigne, acts as a thought leader for the social media industry by maintaining a dedicated blog for his personal and professional posts. He operates under complete transparency to allow his customers, investors, and competitors to see the financial standing of his startup platform and follow his path to success. As customers review the content and interact with Joel, he positions himself as an industry expert who offers valuable information about his field.

Here's an example of Joel's thought leadership in action:

Joel Gascoigne 🌐 @joelgascoigne · 15 Dec 2017
Here are November's @buffer numbers, sharing transparently as I do each month. Feel free to reply with any questions.

Super excited about the foundation we have and all the things that are coming together. 2018 is going to be a very fun year!

	November 2017	Monthly Change	October 2017	Annual Change	November 2016
MRR	$1,367,200	+1.79%	$1,343,220	+32.42%	$1,032,497
ARR	$16,406,400	+1.79%	$16,118,640	+32.42%	$12,389,964
Product					
Customers	78,496	+1.18%	77,579	+21.28%	64,723
Churn Rate	5.26%	-1.50%	5.34%	+4.57%	5.03%
Net Promoter Score	52	+1.96%	51	-7.14%	56
Product Efficiency					
Revenue per Customer	$17.42	+0.60%	$17.31	+9.18%	$15.95
Lifetime Value	$331.13	+2.13%	$324.24	+4.41%	$317.15
Customer Acquisition Cost	$32.79	-2.47%	$33.62	N/A	N/A
Company Health					
Team Size	69	-2.82%	71	-12.86%	79
Revenue per Employee	$237,774	+4.74%	$227,023	+51.61%	$156,835
Bank Balance	$5,211,039	+7.54%	$4,845,897	+181.72%	$1,849,710
Gross Margin	87.85%	-0.06%	87.90%	+1.14%	86.86%
EBITDA Margin	28.27%	+4.32%	27.10%	+184.12%	9.95%

💬 12   🔁 28   ♡ 244

2. Jessica Mah, Founder and CEO of inDinero, positions herself as a thought leader in the financial world by pursuing magazine spots that allow her to share her expertise with a wide audience. She capitalizes on these opportunities by utilizing her skills as a true ambivert. By listening and speaking at the right moments, she can address her audience's needs while putting her MVP out there as a solution to business owner's cash flow and management.

Here's an example of Jessica's thought leadership in action:

3. Elon Musk consistently acts as a thought leader by leading discussions about the future of technology. His progress toward space travel opportunities and fast travel, by way of a "hyperloop," allows him to easily maintain his place as an expert in the field. Musk has acted as a thought leader well before making progress toward those goals, and future startup founders will need to be thought leaders to be successful in their industries.

If you can identify that a startup founder is acting as a thought leader, and utilizing multiple channels to get the word out, give them five points and move on to the next section.

Is There a Clear Understanding of Consumers and Competitors?

The next three points help you determine whether there is a clear understanding of a startup's customers and competitors. The startup must adequately tend to the needs of these two entities now and in the future.

Simply launching a winning MVP with no future plans for updates and upgrades will leave the startup stagnant and out of date in a short amount of time. At the start, the product should not only be remembered for its ability to resolve problems, but also for its ability to beat the competition every step of the way. The product should perform well beyond the standards set by the other products and companies operating within that space. From there, they must be willing to evolve their MVP and business approach to meet the changing interests and needs throughout their niche industry.

Look at how the startup plans to adapt as the demand or need for their product evolves. If they can anticipate and are able to adapt, then award three points to the startup from the Blankenship Valuation Method.

How Fast Does the Startup Respond to Customer Complaints and Requests?

Fast response times are critical in today's business world. Therefore, startup founders who make quick response times a vital aspect of their company operations should earn two points.

Customers expect to receive a quick resolution to their problems with a product, or at least receive an honest response from the founders. Static silence tends to make the customers feel alienated or unheard, which can irreparably damage the startup's reputation and the customer's perception of their product.

To prevent this situation, the Hustler must commit to responding to all customer correspondence within 60 minutes (or less). When startups aim to make things right with the customer, they make that individual feel important and valued as an integral part of the company's success.

Can't Find the Data? Send Out a Personal Request

Even with the most transparent companies, response time data can be difficult to obtain in its raw form. You can act as a customer before investing to see how the product and startup work as a whole.

Before investing, you should directly engage with the MVP to get excited about the product and anticipate the startup's success. As you interact with the product, jot down some likes and dislikes to share with the company founders. Once you share the information, start the clock to see how fast you receive a response. By doing this, you'll gain information about the startup's response times and learn about their customer service quality.

Aiming for Perfection Can Lead to the Startup's Downfall

Providing a response does not mean saying "Yes" to every request. Instead, startup founders must analyze the reasonableness of the request, and then determine how it will impact the bottom line. Not everything can be perfect for customers, especially as the startup and its MVP evolve to meet the needs of its client base.

Sometimes, if a customer's unreasonable requests are taking valuable time away from the startup, they should not engage with that customer ever again. The loss of resources can prove detrimental to a startup, especially in its earliest phases, so knowing when to refuse a request and doing so promptly, can help the company succeed in phenomenal ways. In the end, the ability to juggle resources without using too much energy to satisfy a single customer is the hallmark of a successful startup.

The startup must provide timely responses to earn two points for this section. If responses are inappropriate or take too much time to send out, then the startup does not earn any points for this section.

Does the Startup Utilize Smart Energy Savings Practices?

Energy savings can mean the difference between a startup that becomes the next billion-dollar empire and one that fails in its first year. Startups that can save time and money while channeling energies in the right direction earn five points for this category.

Ross' lesson: use your resources effectively *and* efficiently, otherwise you will waste energy and will not be able to complete tasks that are necessary to win.

Startups must channel their energies to reach key goals and continue marching toward success. Channeling time and effort to the wrong places can leave the founders scrambling to make up for efforts that failed to convert into product sales.

Ask the Right Questions

Analyzing energy savings activities can prove difficult as you look at the startup from the outside in. You must be able to take a close look at the startup's operations to determine how well they utilize their time. To accomplish this goal, start asking all the right questions while meeting with startup founders.

Open up the dialogue about how the founders achieve each phase of their operations while focusing on saving time and money in the long run.

Here are examples of what you should ask the founders:

- Do you attend paid conferences and events?

- How often do you attend startup happy hour?

- How often are you updating your product?

Inquire if they regularly interact with their customers and respond to requests in a timely manner or are they using their time for less lucrative activities, like redundant company meetings?

You should be able to see whether the startup is always efficient with its time, and thus more worthy of an investment.

For Energy Savings Analyzation, Transparency is Key

Transparency allows investors to easily evaluate energy savings practices utilized by startups of all kinds. Joel, from Buffer, employs this method to allow potential investors, customers, and competitors alike to see just how well he uses his key resources.

By maintaining complete transparency using the Baremetrics platform, Joel allows investors and the general public to see where the company allocates its money. Every dollar spent by the startup is displayed in all its glory with live updates through this innovative platform. As you look at the financial data for Buffer, you can see whether Buffer is spending its money wisely.

The next page shows an example of how transparent Buffer is vis-à-vis an investor update sent to me by Joel in October of 2017:

Hi Ross,

I'm happy to share our metrics for end of October:

	October 2017	Monthly Change	September 2017	Annual Change	October 2016
MRR	$1,343,220	+2.33%	$1,312,614	+33.52%	$1,005,986
ARR	$16,118,640	+2.33%	$15,751,368	+33.52%	$12,071,832
Product					
Customers	77,579	+1.69%	76,293	+27.55%	60,276
Churn Rate	5.34%	-2.91%	5.50%	+11.25%	4.80%
Net Promoter Score	51	+0.00%	51	-8.93%	56
Product Efficiency					
Revenue per Customer	$17.31	+0.64%	$17.20	+4.68%	$16.69
Lifetime Value	$324.24	+3.65%	$312.82	-5.90%	$347.70
Customer Acquisition Cost	$33.62	-5.75%	$35.67	N/A	N/A
Company Health					
Team Size	71	-1.39%	72	-10.13%	79
Revenue per Employee	$227,023.10	+3.77%	$218,769.00	+48.57%	$152,808
Bank Balance	$4,845,897	+10.96%	$4,367,158	+169.07%	$1,800,963
Gross Margin	87.90%	+0.34%	87.60%	+0.93%	87.09%
EBITDA Margin	27.10%	+3.71%	26.13%	+69.59%	15.98%

I'm happy to welcome our newest investor, Purpose Ventures, as a shareholder. They have recently finalized a transaction with Leo. Purpose Ventures are now Buffer's 3rd largest investor, representing 1.6% of outstanding ownership.

Looking back on Q3, we made great progress on several fronts. Those accomplishments as well as future vision and strategy were written up in a recent Transparency Report.

Happy Thanksgiving to all US folks!

- Joel

If the startups you're considering are not being transparent, ask to see more financial data, such as monthly account statements and official tax returns. Explore the various methods they use to create their products, become thought leaders and support their customer base.

If you notice any issues with the way they spend their time and money, you should write a check to a different startup and not theirs.

Can the Startup **CAPTURE** *Traction to Become the Next Billion-Dollar Empire?*

Once you made it through the traction section of the Blankenship Valuation Method, you can then look back to see how a great process leads to excellent traction.

The process section builds up a core team and automated product that supports the acquisition of evangelical followers. As the core team of founders fulfills their role of Hacker, Hustler and Growth Hacker, they boost their startup's ability to respond to phenomenal growth as it develops. The automation of the product has the same effect by ensuring the process can scale as the startup company grows and thrives in their industry.

A startup that fulfills the requirements of these five areas will earn the full 20 points for the traction phase of the Blankenship Valuation Method. When combined with the other two aspects of the CAPTURE acronym, the startup has the potential to be awarded 40 points from process and traction.

6

Financials
The Structure and Control of Winning Startups

"If you don't understand the details of your business you are going to fail."

-Jeff Bezos

The final step in the Blankenship Valuation Method focuses on financials with the most important concepts being: economic structure and control. The last 12 possible points of our 100-point formula centers around not only startup's financial factors but also the founders' knowledge of these financial terms and metrics.

The startup needs to score 90 points in the Blankenship Valuation Method as the bare minimum to receive an investment. Therefore, these 12 points from financials are critical in determining whether the startup receives funding. Exploring the startup's structure and control will also help you determine if the founders are prepared for the continued growth required to take their company to the next level.

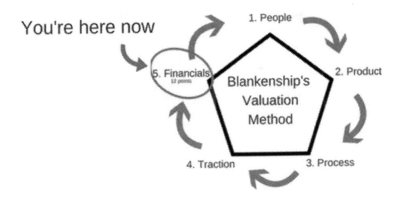

Control and Structure Help Prepare Startups for Accelerated Growth

As an investor, this chapter will teach you about winning financial structures and control that will help you determine if the startup will make the best use of all their investment capital and continue their trajectory of upward, sustainable growth for years to come. If the startup displays the right combination of financial understanding and planning metrics in the earliest stages, you can rest assure that the founders have a better chance at becoming the next billion-dollar company.

For startups founders, this chapter will explore structure and control mechanisms that investors look for when determining the valuation of a company. As a startup, the way you handle the planning process will have a significant impact on your ability to secure capital from your investors at any stage of your journey. When you align your financials toward the best practices, you're also proving to investors that your startup is worth investing in.

To become a billion-dollar empire, startup founders must align their operations with the financial requirements that all great companies meet in their earliest stages. At the root of these considerations, you will find the base concepts that matter the most to the founding team and then move onto the most important economic structure and control factors.

The Two Most Important Concepts for Investors and Entrepreneurs: Economics and Control

When it comes down to the most important base concepts, investors and entrepreneurs have to align views to ensure both people receive the most value for their time and money.

1. Economics of the Deal

The economics of the deal reveals how the startup founders and their investors will come out ahead as the company increases its value. At its core, the economics of the deal involve understanding how much money an investor is putting into the startup in exchange for a certain amount of equity.

2. Startup Control

The board members that have the most control over the startup have the most influence in determining the future of the company. Of the many control documents required for successful enterprises, startups must have the following prepared and organized properly before launching:

- Articles of Incorporation
- Corporate Bylaws
- Corporate Ledger
- Employee Agreements
- Term Sheet and Subscription Agreement
- Board Member Election Consent
- Plan for Liquidity Event

Ross' Lesson: if you need help with any of these crucial documents, get more information on our website AngelKings.com/Advisors

These seven factors help establish who is in control of the startup through every growth stage. Having these documents formalized, well before the seed stage, gives the startup an edge over the competition as they attempt to procure investment capital. Investors should inquire about these documents and be prepared to walk away from the deal if the control factors do not properly align with that startup.

Raising Money and Investing

Both founders and investors need to understand how much is going into the deal and how much value will be generated by the time you reach an IPO. With the right level of capital, will the startup become the next billion-dollar empire? It shouldn't be about getting rich fast. Both startup founders and investors often have deeper reasons for continuing down their chosen paths. The investment capital facilitates continued operations for both sides.

Startup founders raise money to help their business dreams become a reality. The most important reason for raising these funds is to help scale and grow the company. A founder may have started with little to no funds and need to raise capital to keep moving toward the completion of an in-demand MVP with a fully-fledged process. Their final goal may center around resolving a problem with their proven product and expanding to claim a majority of the market share in the process.

Investors, on the other hand, are optimistic that their investments will pay off in the end. They must practice their due diligence in distributing their investment funds to make sure the money goes to the startups that have the best chance at making it big. By receiving great returns from their investment dollars, these investors can continue impacting future generations by supporting their startups from the ground up.

When core concepts are understood and shared by investors and founders, everyone can work together to pave the way to success. For every startup, it is important to recognize where the money is coming from and how it is being spent because these are key to establishing a profitable pathway.

Money Pathways: Where is it Coming from and Where is it Going?

As part of the financial valuation process, it is vital that you identify and resolve the concerns that surround the contribution and acquisition of investment capital. Tracing the money pathways by identifying where it is coming from and where it is headed will help investors and founders work towards success together.

These questions should be asked, answered, and understood by startup founders well before they begin raising capital.

Who are the Investors?

Although investment capital can come from anyone with cash to invest, the most value comes from receiving investments from thought leaders and mentors in your startup's industry. Who are the people you look up to in your industry? As you achieve great success, who do you wish to emulate along the way?

When your trusted advisors provide investment funds for your company, they may act as valuable contributors through each stage of success. For example, you could offer a 5% equity to a board member in exchange for marketing, fundraising,

Ross' Lesson: find industry leaders who promote your startup in exchange for vested equity over time.

and operational expertise. A startup can utilize equity in many ways to create a symmetry of interests between the founder and key advisors.

What are the Terms?

Giving too little, or too much, away during the seed round and other investment stages can threaten the financial health of your startup in startling ways. Retaining enough control of your startup, while giving your investors enough equity will become one of your greatest challenges and balancing acts.

Without achieving balance, your startup could end up under the control of investors who do not share the same vision of success as your founding team. This could lead to problems down the road. Therefore, it is important to retain enough equity amongst the founding team to ensure that you still have a stake in the company in future rounds.

Ross' Lesson: founders and investors should negotiate a quick, clean, simple deal so that each can go back to focusing on what's most important: building a profitable company.

Where Should I Raise Capital?

Knowing where to look for capital funds makes a big difference in the success of your startup. Startups who raise money just through friends and family rarely become a billion-dollar empire.

Instead, look for investors who are thought leaders and mentors in your vertical market space. When you have well-respected thought leaders on your company board, your company earns instant credibility in the

Ross' Lesson: when looking for investors, look for thought leaders who are reputable and have experience in your industry.

industry while enjoying mentorship opportunities every step of the way.

Peter Thiel had a number of huge successes before investing in Facebook. He co-founded Paypal, founded Clarium Capital, is chairman of Palantir Technologies, and launched Founders Fund. His many successes proved useful in helping Facebook grow to become what it is today.

When Should I Raise Funds?

Although it may feel tempting to stockpile funds in case your startup faces adverse market conditions or other revenue-impacting situations, it is not wise to raise capital until you absolutely need it. When you patiently raise capital, you are telling your potential investors that you are only looking for smart money that is thoughtful and focused on creating a profitable business versus raising capital just because you can.

Ross' Lesson: look for startups that are too busy acquiring new customers instead of the ones that are constantly trying to raise money.

Again, when you do end up raising money from your trusted advisors, you should limit your fundraising efforts strictly to the amount that is needed to grow your company.

Why Do I Need to Raise Money?

If you have a proven product and a great structure, you may wonder why you need to raise money. Can't you just retain all the equity in the company and continue along as you have been? The answer is yes; if you never intend to scale your empire into a billion-dollar enterprise.

To fund future growth that will allow you to expand your startup and scale the automated delivery of your MVP, you must secure smart investment capital. Also, the acquisition of investments from industry leaders will give you incredible value beyond the power of the dollar. You will also be able to enjoy continued mentorship from thought leaders who are fully invested in the success of your company.

Ross' Lesson: startups need to decide how big they want to grow. Do they want to be a lifestyle business, medium-sized company, or a unicorn with real wings?

How Can I Negotiate the Best Deal?

Successfully negotiating the best deal depends on your ability to listen to and understand the concerns of your investors and members of your founding team. Channel your inner-ambivert as you forge ahead into the negotiation process.

How Transparency Makes Financial Valuation Easy for Investors

In most cases, full transparency allows investors to explore the value of a startup while developing immense trust in the founding team. When Joel created Buffer, he decided to make his whole operation transparent from the start, including the financial metrics for his growing company. In addition to the information posted on his personal blog, he set up a revenue dashboard on the Baremetrics platform.

The platform allows investors, clients, and even competitors to follow the revenue growth of Buffer every step of the way. With just a glance, you can see a dozen revealing financial metrics, including monthly recurring revenue (MRR), net revenue, fees, user churn rate, and average revenue per user. With everything on the table, Joel has created a sense of trust not only with Buffer's client base, but with his early investors too.

Joel's track record of sustainable, scalable growth highlights the fact that full transparency *does not* negatively impact the potential success of a startup. In fact, it has the opposite effect, as it allows potential investors to predict future growth and success of the Buffer platform. Continuing on the current growth trajectory will allow Buffer to easily become the next billion-dollar empire in the future.

Although startup founders must set out to answer the money pathway questions before raising money, investors need to consider similar questions before providing funds to any startup. In the end, the founders' answers to these concerns, not the startup's, will play a vital role in the final element of the **Blankenship Valuation Method.**

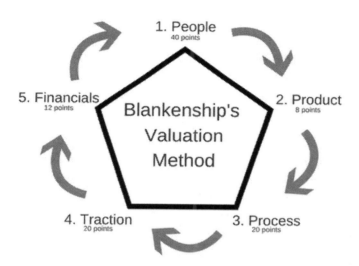

Questions to Ask When Applying the Valuation Method for Financials

As an investor, you must ask questions that not only protect your bottom line, but also allow you to receive great returns from these startups. You must continue to objectively assign a value to the startup's main elements.

To complete the process of applying the Blankenship Valuation Method, you must answer the **three following questions** about the financial structure and control of the startup in which you're considering investing. These three areas add up to 12 points total, completing the 100 point spread for the valuation process.

1. Do the Founders Understand Their Financial Status and Needs? (2 pts.)

When you evaluated the company's founders, it's unlikely that you considered their financial knowledge and understanding - now is the time to do just that.

Although determining the founder's financial knowledge might appear to be subjective, I've found these questions to be as important as any others you might want to ask.

A founding team with a clear understanding of the startup's financial status and needs will be better able to respond to the changing dynamics through periods of scalable growth. Otherwise, the founding team may struggle to maintain control of the finances as their company gains traction and grows into a billion-dollar empire.

Therefore, you should ask the startup founders tough questions about their understanding of pertinent financial terms, such as cash flow, expenses, convertible notes and profit/loss reports. Explore their financial knowledge from concepts of how they will reach profitability to their path toward a significant liquidity event. If they can answer your questions about financials, give the startup two points for this section.

2. What Does the Term Sheet Reveal About Economics and Control? (8 pts.)

The term sheet presented by the startup founders will reveal an immense amount of information about the economics and control of their company. When you utilize my valuation metrics, you should expect to secure a reasonable deal during the negotiations.

To ensure you are obtaining a great deal, you must determine if the valuation numbers indicate that you will have enough stake in the company to exhibit control in the best and worst of times. However, you will also need to achieve a balance. The amount of stake and control you hold should remain reasonable to ensure the founders retain interest and drive in increasing the success of their startup. If the term sheet reveals excellent economic and control factors, award the startup the full eight points for this section.

3. Where Should I Invest My Capital? (2 pts.)

Unlike the previous elements within the Blankenship Valuation Method, the last two points will take a look at you, as the investor, rather than the startup's people, product, process, traction, and financials.

When looking for investment opportunities, you should always focus on the industries and market spaces that you know well. With startups looking for investors who can act as mentors for their continued success, ask yourself if you can act as a thought leader and offer mentorship through your role on the Board. You should be available to interact with the startup at least once a month after you've invested in that startup.

If you can act as a thought leader and be available at least once a month, then award two more points to complete the valuation process.

Once you finish the financials section of the Blankenship Valuation Method, review the other areas and add up your totals to see how many points the startup earned.

At the seed round, you can contribute up to $20 million dollars to startups that have scored at least 90 points. The score requirements increase to 95, 97 and 99 in subsequent rounds. Only the best startups can receive all 100 points from the Blankenship Valuation Method – and at that point, they are billion-dollar companies, not startups anymore.

Here are the primary fundraising stages and how many points it needs to have to receive funding at that level:

get to 100,

Seed Stage = 90 Points

get ## Series A funding = 95 points

2 billion # ## Series B funding = 97 points

Series C funding = 99 points

Although you can confidently move forward with startups that score 90 points or higher, you must explore supporting factors to ensure your investment will yield large returns in the long run.

Weigh Other Factors to Determine if the Startup Measures Up to the Blankenship Standard

Protecting your finances should remain a top priority as you take a chance in backing startups that score high during the valuation stage. To ensure you have the best chance at success, you must consider timing, overall value, and negotiation tactics surrounding the investment process.

Fortune Favors the Bold

Timing is everything when it comes to making great strides as an angel and startup investor. You are coming in at the earliest stages to support the projected growth of a promising company. Although you are taking a risk by jumping in at the early stages, you could potentially reap amazing returns on your investments. If you do your due diligence by applying the Blankenship Valuation Method, you have less to worry about from an investor standpoint.

At this point, go through the Blankenship Valuation Method to determine if the startup reaches the required 90 points for the seed round. Once you determine that the startup is a good fit and projects phenomenal growth in the coming years, it is time to invest and stake your claim on the rewards well before the company hits the public stage.

Understand the Value of Investing in Startups

When you invest in public companies, you have the chance at obtaining small returns without playing a role in the success of the company. However, investing in startups allow you to net even higher returns while making a huge difference in the success of future generations who enter that market.

Your potential returns as a startup investor will almost always beat the returns from the S&P Index every year, which annualizes around 7% to 10% growth. Your payoff in impacting the success of future generations might be the biggest reward for investing in startups.

How to Negotiate the Best Deal for Great Investment Returns

The negotiation stage of the investment process allows you to obtain the best deal and receive positive returns each year. The economic and control factors must properly align to showcase the startup's skills in money management in the face of growth. If the factors do not properly line up, you should be willing to walk away until they do.

Here are Three Tips to Negotiate the Best Investment Deals:

1. Make it less about the money and more about how much value you will bring to the startup. Beyond writing a check, speak directly with the founders via phone and describe your past experiences in their industry, give examples of how you can, and will, help the startup become a billion-dollar company.

2. Meet with the startup founders in-person. Far too often, most business negotiations and startup investments occur via email. This impersonal, clichéd form of communication, prevents you the investor from getting to really know the founding team. You should aim to make it impossible for the startup to say "no" to your investment; by establishing in-person rapport that goes beyond electronic communication, your odds of doing so will increase substantially.

3. Know that most top startups are busy and they aren't searching for money. Just like the pretty boy or girl you always wanted to ask out to the prom in high school, but they always seemed to have a boyfriend or girlfriend already.... well, the best startups I've ever invested were not seeking investor money. Rather, I

had to source these startups through my extensive network and even cold-call these founders to tell them the value-add I could bring alongside my investment dollars. Here's the challenge with that: when someone knows you're interested, the terms get more difficult. So you have to know what to say when first reaching out through a cold-call or through your network.

Here are examples of what you can say to Founders:

- "My name is Ross Blankenship, I'm calling you because our fund has just a bit more capital to deploy this year, and we think your startup would be perfect for our investment."
- "Even though you might not *need* the money, I will personally make sure that your startup is ready for prime time after this investment."
- "My approach to investing is that you the founder are in charge, and I'm just on-call for you 24/7 should you ever need help."

Negotiating the best deal requires patience, persistence, and the ability to humble yourself. Just because you can write a check to a startup, doesn't mean millions more like you couldn't do the same thing. My approach will help you stand out more, become noticed, and allow you the opportunity to invest in the next billion-dollar startups... that often do not need your money.

Timing is Critical

With timing remaining one of the most important factors when it comes to identifying the next billion-dollar company, you will benefit from determining if the MVP in question aligns with current needs and expectations.

Innovation is great, but the first product to charge out of the gate as a solution to an identified problem is not always the best investment. Great startups tend to learn from the mistakes of the competitors.

Let's look at Facebook again, it wasn't the first social media platform, but it gained traction and overthrew MySpace and Friendster. There is no value in investing in a clone, but Facebook was innovative and brought new features that people loved, such as the usage of real identities or a relationship status.

The product should act as a timeless solution to a problem affecting a massive user base. The startup should have a plan that helps the product evolve to meet the ever-changing needs of their user base without losing sight of their original goals and purpose.

The market needs to support the development and sales of the MVP without too much competition taking market share. The startup should slowly weed out their lesser competitors by releasing a product and an automated delivery system that better serves its purpose than similar items in that market space.

Obtain Investment Funds by Ensuring Your Valuation Remains Reasonable

Startup founders ready to pursue investment funds should complete the valuation process for their own company before pitching to investors. By verifying that your startup has a reasonable valuation, or by being able to justify your startup's valuation, you can streamline the acquisition of investment capital without wasting your or your potential investors' time.

To appropriately value your startup, go through each stage of the Blankenship Valuation Method, from people to financials, to receive your score. Although it will be difficult to remain unbiased, being highly objective will give you a more accurate score.

Next, run some comparisons against other startups in your realm to see how well those entities are performing. When doing a comparative analysis, make sure the companies are serving a similar customer base and delivering the same type of products, doing so will make sure that your comparisons are accurate.

Ross' Lesson: if you want to obtain your startup's valuation, be sure to visit AngelKings.com/Advisors

Finally, run the numbers to determine accurate growth forecasts. You should be able to demonstrate reasonable, scalable growth patterns in the past that will continue through your company's future growth. The forecasts should showcase your company's ability to increase revenues and gain new customers acquisitions by 5% to 10% per month every year.

Verify Official Tax Returns

Verify all tax returns and financial data before investing in a startup. Even if the startup has only existed for months, get access to their Quickbooks, Xero, or inDinero, whichever accounting platform the startup utilizes. If the startup is early (i.e. less than 12 months old), then make sure you have ample access to ensure these filings are happening and that the startup is up-to-date on all financial records. Then within the financials themselves, look to see whether their pitch deck financials match what has, or will be, reported to the IRS. I always employ a "trust but verify" model of accounting, particularly when a startup or early-stage company begins. Though they might say they're not up-to-date on financials, it's your job as an investor to make sure that these financials are accurate with what they pitched you on, and further that they have someone helping them on regular basis with these financials. Based on you reading our book, and watching our full course on financials (AngelKings.com/Course), you should know what you're looking for with any financial data that is presented to you.

Some of the **biggest things you'll find** from analyzing a startup's Balance statements, Profit and Loss statements, and Cash Flow reports are:

- Whether or not the gross revenue is accurate from what you've already been told vis-a-vis the pitch deck.
- Whether or not the margins discussed in the pitch deck are real.
- Whether or not the expenses and costs of payroll such as salaries for full-time employees (founders and early employees) and 1099 independent contractors, are too high and should be reined in before you invest.
- If the startup has more than one year of financial data, you can determine if the startup is increasing revenue while becoming more efficient with COGS (Cost of Goods Sold).

- Whether or not the startup is in need of financial help and is even set-up properly for accurate reporting to the IRS, and you the investor.

Overall, remember that the numbers tell a story. The flow of money, to and from somewhere, starts with proper accounting and financial reporting. If a startup isn't set-up for smart reporting and accounting, they're highly unlikely to report to you the investor, post-investment. And when a startup goes cold and never reports their financials in a transparent, accurate way to investors, it's the biggest red flag of any in this book.

Founders and Investors: an Alignment for Complete Market Success

When investors and founders share the same interests and work toward a common goal, their ability to build the next billion-dollar empire increases substantially. In the end, both sides of the equation want to build value in the company and enjoy the spoils as the liquidity event finally occurs.

In the next section, you will explore financial structure and control metrics in depth to better understand this important aspect of angel and startup investing.

7

Financing the Company
The Pathway to Great Returns for Investors and Founders

"Sweat equity is the most valuable equity there is. Know your business and industry better than anyone else in the world. Love what you do or don't do it."

-Mark Cuban

Laying the right foundation from the start gives founders the tools and knowledge they will need to successfully fundraise and grow their company. Startups should begin by creating its structure as a C corporation, or "C-Corp," and then establishing the bylaws, equity structure and vesting plan that will allow for a simplified fundraising process. Also, founders must understand how to create term sheets and purchase agreements that align their interests with potential investors and facilitate a move toward the creation of a billion-dollar empire.

Throughout this chapter on financing the company, we will explore the structural and financial elements that play a vital role in the establishment of a startup that can attract investments through every round – from seed to series A, all the way to an IPO.

A Startup's Structure Can Open Doors to Phenomenal Success

Before a startup can work towards the acquisition of capital by attracting investments from you and other likeminded investors, they must create a structure that benefits all parties. Although founders need to have a singular edge in the creation and delivery of their MVP, their company structure must follow a predictable formula to draw in investors. The formula revolves around the proper creation of corporate documents, establishment as a C-Corp, and development of a reasonable equity structure and vesting plan. As an investor, performing your due diligence centers around your ability to verify that the startup has the right structure from day one.

Ross' Lesson: a well-organized startup tends to correlate to one that will eventually give awesome investor updates and keep investors apprised.

The Creation of Corporate Documents

Although modifications can occur at any time, the corporate documents created early on will follow the startup through every investment round. Before you can confidently jump onboard as an investor, the startup should have the following documents created, filed, and presented to you:

- Articles of Incorporation (preferably in Delaware, Nevada or Wyoming)
- IRS Employer Identification Number
- Bylaws and Board of Directors' Documents
- Equity Structure and Vesting Plan
- Employment Agreements (including those with the founders)

:ation of these documents will prepare the founders scalable growth of their company. For startups, a great founaation starts with the process of filing the Articles of Incorporation.

Inc. Vs. LLC: Establishing an Excellent Foundation

Although LLC structured companies have their place in the business world, startups looking to secure capital from investors, like you, need to establish themselves as a Delaware C-Corp. The vast majority of startups that go public and become billion-dollar empires all use the Delaware C-Corp structure because Delaware offers a more business friendly legal and operational environment to begin companies.

1. To establish this type of enterprise, startup founders must file Articles of Incorporation using an affordable service, such as "Valcu." Valcu is a platform that helps with startup incorporation and corporate management. By using an affordable service, founders can file their paperwork without having to pay out large sums for attorneys.
2. Before filing, it is important for founders to pick a non-trademarked name by ensuring their selection does not show up on the United States Patent and Trademark Office website at USPTO.gov. Make sure you conduct a thorough search to determine whether or not there are any trademark or patent issues related to your startup's name or brand.
3. Then, founders need to establish a single class of stock, assign a nominal value and create a release of liability for the future Board of Directors.
4. Founders should complete this process early on in the establishment of their startup to get the ball rolling on their path to success. You can modify the information included any time after filing, so there is no drawback to completing this process early.

5. Founders will usually receive their Articles of Incorporation paperwork within a week after filing, though the process can be expedited for an extra fee. While waiting for the paperwork, founders should focus on developing their bylaws.

Development of Bylaws for the Startup

Well before startups begin the fundraising process, the founders need to focus on creating their bylaws document that spells out how their company will run. The bylaws cover the name of the company, founding members, the Board of Directors, committee type, officers, meetings, conflicts of interest and amendments typically in a five to 30-page document. This document will include details about the frequency and content of company meetings along with the role and structural changes that

Ross' Lesson: examples of founding documents can be found on our website at AngelKings.com/Advisors

come with the startup's growth.

This important document offers the founding team the structure they need to work toward scalable growth well into the future. The last item on the agenda is the creation of an equity structure and vesting plan that appeals to the founding team members and their future investors.

Create and Follow a Beneficial Equity Structure and Vesting Plan

While you are looking for startups to invest in, verify that their equity structure and vesting plan makes sense and remains reasonable through every round of funding.

A reasonable equity structure and vesting plan allow founders to reap the rewards for their hard work while making room for future investors and employees. A great equity structure helps ensure founders stick with their startup until they can reach their ideal liquidity event by merging, selling or going public. Creating an excellent vesting plan, such as one with a one-year cliff and four-year vesting schedule, will incentivize the founders to work with the company long-term.

The way the team initially splits their equity also matters. Although the founding team may want to split the equity evenly amongst themselves, a purely equitable division of stock/shares can backfire in the long run. Instead, founders should proportion equity based on a meritocracy by reflecting on their contributions of either monetary capital or "sweat equity." The latter contribution (sweat equity) is a person's non-monetary contribution, which often involves hard work, late nights, and extreme dedication to the startup.

You want founders that value sweat equity as much as cash. Always avoid startups with a 50/50 equity allocation, which are when founders own completely equal shares for a company, because those arrangements are problematic as the company grows. If any founders walk away from the startup before fully vesting, they should lose their potential for future gains and only take what they have earned up to that point. You leave, you lose; it's that simple.

Also, remember that cash is king! The founding team should retain a portion of their capital for materials and equipment, employee acquisition, and other sources of growth, rather than spending it all on salaries. In fact, the founding team should earn a fraction of what they are worth, as their greatest payout will arrive when their company hits the big time by going public or being acquired.

Term Sheet Creation Tactics that Help Win Investments in Every Round

All great investment negotiations start with the presentation of the term sheet. This non-binding document brings the economics and control together through the establishment of rules for securities and the creation of the rights that come with each investment.

The best term sheets are simple, negotiable documents that are easy for investors to understand. Therefore, the term sheet should have no option pool, legal fees, expiration or confidentiality clause and remain standardized for all investors.

Ross' Lesson: term sheets should be negotiated in 30 days or less, otherwise, they are too complicated.

Even though the term sheet is a "non-binding" agreement between parties - the investor and the startup entrepreneur - knowing these three following rules will help all sides reach a mutually favorable agreement.

Ross' Three Crucial Rules for Term Sheets:

1.) Valuation matters. Both investors and startups need to understand the valuation, i.e., stock purchase price.

For investors, know that the term sheet's stock purchase price is a starting place from which you can negotiate a better deal. An investor shouldn't look at the purchase price the same way you would if you were buying a publicly-traded company's stock. You should evaluate the stock purchase price based on the fundamentals you've learned in this book, i.e., People, Product, Process, Traction, and Financials.

And if you don't understand the proposed purchase price or the startup's valuation, and cannot explain it to others, don't invest.

For startup entrepreneurs, your valuation in whatever round you're raising will set the tone for all future rounds. Now's the chance to set a reasonable valuation (of course, using the Blankenship Valuation Model) and justifying the price with metrics and data that shows you've validated your startup's model. If you don't set a reasonable valuation that leaves room for an "up-round" or a higher future valuation, you can seriously impair your ability to raise in the future... so be smart about your startup's official valuation!

2.) Control. Who's in charge?

Knowing how much control and which rights an investor receives, is critical for all parties.

For investors, if you want a more hands-on approach and more control in terms of how the startup is run, and you plan on investing more than other investors in whatever round (Seed, Series A, B, and so forth) make sure the term sheet contains investor rights that gives you a board seat. It's not necessary, but can be beneficial if you believe your experience would be conducive to the startup. You should also consider a small amount of "protective provisions." These provisions can include restrictions on how much debt a startup should take on as well as anti-dilution provisions on the company's stock... i.e. how many new shares can be issued to future investors.

For startup entrepreneurs, you will want to ensure that your startup isn't being micromanaged and that the control and protective provisions are limited. Yes, you should be open to some control provisions, particularly if an investor is planning a bigger role - and more capital infused - into the company, but limit these provisions so it won't inhibit your startup's future fundraising rounds.

3.) Set a 30-day timeline and deadline for the term sheet.

Don't raise in perpetuity. Doing so will make your startup lose its focus. Rather the focus should always be on building a great team, product, and all the other critical factors from the Blankenship Valuation Method.

For investors, ensure that the term sheet deadline is 30 days or less. Your time is valuable, and you need to make the startup a priority as well. If you're planning on investing and have used the Blankenship Valuation Method to reach an investment decision, you should be able to agree to a term sheet in less than a week, and certainly less than 30 days. Don't waste your time, nor the startups. A startup's life can be short, and time is too precious.

For startup entrepreneurs, because you should be focusing on the core principles of building your business and driving revenue, a 30-day window is equally beneficial to you as well. The deadline on a term sheet should be the one binding feature of the entire document. Make it happen, quickly!

The Big No's: Option Pool, Legal Fees, Expiration, and Confidentiality

The founding team benefits from term sheets with less restrictions in place.

1. The lack of terms for an **option pool** allows founders to simply establish their equity split and vesting agreement.

2. **Legal fees** should not come up as a part of the term sheet either, as that ties up capital that could otherwise be used to help the startup grow.
3. Term sheets should have a specific day and time in which an investment is to be finalized so that the investment decision doesn't drag-on needlessly without end.
4. Founders and investors alike should retain the ability to explore their options freely to ensure everyone comes on board during the purchase agreement signing stage.
5. Founders should not customize their term sheets for each investor, because having a standardized document will result in energy savings that benefit the startup and their investors.

Although establishing complete control seems like a smart move at first glance, overly complicated or limiting term sheets are not beneficial to you as an investor nor the founding team, so they should be avoided at all costs.

A Close Look at What Matters Most to Investors

As an investor looking for the best deals, you have to objectively analyze the term sheet to see if you are receiving the most value for your investment dollars. Pay close attention to the details that involve the valuation, ownership, and pro rata rights sections to determine whether or not you are receiving an excellent deal in the earliest rounds of fundraising. Valuation covers the total price for securities and how much equity you will receive for your investment.

Ross' Lesson: always
negotiate as much equity as
you can, but keep in mind
that founders need to be
incentivized to continue
growing the company.

The ownership section will reveal how much stake you will receive in exchange for your investment in each round. Balance is important here, as you want the founders to retain enough stake to remain committed to the success of their startup, but you also want to receive a great return on your investment.

Pro rata rights open the door for future investments that increase your stake in the company through each subsequent round. By securing this right, you can minimize dilution of your ownership percentage as more investors come onboard.

The next section allows you to analyze the contents of a term sheet that can benefit both startup founders and you as their investor.

ers: This is a Term Sheet. Know it well.

nice reference (handwritten annotation)

TERM SHEET
FOR SERIES A PREFERRED STOCK FINANCING OF
[INSERT COMPANY NAME], INC.
[____ __, 20__]

This Term Sheet summarizes the principal terms of the Series A Preferred Stock Financing of [_____], Inc., a [Delaware] corporation (the "**Company**"). In consideration of the time and expense devoted and to be devoted by the Investors with respect to this investment, the No Shop/Confidentiality [and Counsel and Expenses] provisions of this Term Sheet shall be binding obligations of the Company whether or not the financing is consummated. No other legally binding obligations will be created until definitive agreements are executed and delivered by all parties. This Term Sheet is not a commitment to invest, and is conditioned on the completion of due diligence, legal review and documentation that is satisfactory to the Investors. This Term Sheet shall be governed in all respects by the laws of [_____the].[1]

Offering Terms

Closing Date:	As soon as practicable following the Company's acceptance of this Term Sheet and satisfaction of the Conditions to Closing (the "**Closing**"). [*provide for multiple closings if applicable*]
Investors:	Investor No. 1: [_____] shares ([__]%), $[_____]
	Investor No. 2: [_____] shares ([__]%), $[_____]
	[as well other investors mutually agreed upon by Investors and the Company]
Amount Raised:	$[_____], [including $[_____] from the conversion of principal [and interest] on bridge notes].[2]
Price Per Share:	$[_____] per share (based on the capitalization of the Company set forth below) (the "**Original Purchase Price**").
Pre-Money Valuation:	The Original Purchase Price is based upon a fully-diluted pre-money valuation of $[_____] and a fully-diluted post-money valuation of $[_____] (including an employee pool representing [__]% of the fully-diluted post-money capitalization).
Capitalization:	The Company's capital structure before and after the Closing is set forth on Exhibit A.

Again, the term sheet is a non-binding document that provides the foundation for startup founders and investors to negotiate an investment at any round. The sample above shows the economics and valuation part of the term sheet. The sample on the next page displays investor rights and the control portion of the term sheet.

Control: Who's in charge

Voting Rights:	The Series A Preferred shall vote together with the Common Stock on an as-converted basis, and not as a separate class, except (i) [so long as *[insert fixed number, or %, or "any"]* shares of Series A Preferred are outstanding,] the Series A Preferred as a class shall be entitled to elect [_____] [()] members of the Board (the "**Series A Directors**"), and (ii) as required by law. The Company's Certificate of Incorporation will provide that the number of authorized shares of Common Stock may be increased or decreased with the approval of a majority of the Preferred and Common Stock, voting together as a single class, and without a separate class vote by the Common Stock.[6]
Protective Provisions:	[So long as *[insert fixed number, or %, or "any"]* shares of Series A Preferred are outstanding,] in addition to any other vote or approval required under the Company's Charter or Bylaws, the Company will not, without the written consent of the holders of at least [__]% of the Company's Series A Preferred, either directly or by amendment, merger, consolidation, or otherwise:

    (i) liquidate, dissolve or wind-up the affairs of the Company, or effect any merger or consolidation or any other Deemed Liquidation Event; (ii) amend, alter, or repeal any provision of the Certificate of Incorporation or Bylaws [in a manner adverse to the Series A Preferred];[7] (iii) create or authorize the creation of or issue any other security convertible into or exercisable for any equity security, having rights, preferences or privileges senior to or on parity with the Series A Preferred, or increase the authorized number of shares of Series A Preferred; (iv) purchase or redeem or pay any dividend on any capital stock prior to the Series A Preferred, [other than stock repurchased from former employees or consultants in connection with the cessation of their employment/services, at the lower of fair market value or cost;] [other than as approved by the Board, including the approval of [_____] Series A Director(s)]; or (v) create or authorize the creation of any debt security [if the Company's aggregate indebtedness would exceed $[____][other than equipment leases or bank lines of credit][unless such debt security has received the prior approval of the Board of Directors, including the approval of [_____] Series A Director(s)]; (vi) create or hold capital stock in any subsidiary that is not a wholly-owned subsidiary or dispose of any subsidiary stock or all or substantially all of any subsidiary assets; [or (vii) increase or decrease the size of the Board of Directors].[8]

Term Sheet Evaluation: Does it Fulfill the Needs of Both Parties?

There are two key parts of the term sheet. The first part explores securities and valuation, while the second covers the rights of the investors. Although the term sheet is non-binding, the purchase agreement should closely align with the original wording from the term sheet, unless negotiations resulted in changes approved by all parties. The valuation section details the investment round, type of stock, pre-money and post-money value of the startup, amount of offering, liquidity event preferences, dividends and general voting rights.

Investors must carefully review the term sheet to ensure it makes sense from an economic standpoint before moving onto the next stage of the investment process. You should pay close attention to the valuation figures and liquidation preference, because these two terms will provide an opportunity for return on investment.

Pre-Money and Post-Money Valuation Figures

The pre-money and post-money valuation figures allow you to determine the value of the startup and see if the economics of the deal make sense for all parties. To find these two figures, you will need to find the post-money valuation by dividing the venture capital investment by the ownership percentage. You can then find the pre-money valuation of the startup by taking the post-money valuation and subtracting the venture capital investments.

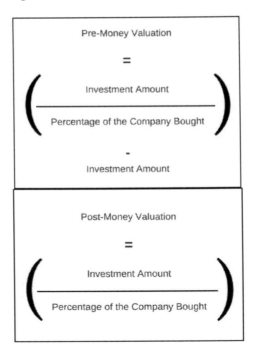

Liquidation Preference

The liquidation preference determines the payout order and how much investors get paid in the case of a liquidation event, such as an IPO, merger, or sale of the company. The liquidation event covers the actions that will occur when the startup reaches their liquidity event. You can assign a multiple to this section that allows you to receive one to ten times your investment dollars back when the startup changes hands or goes public. Identifying your liquidation preference can also come into play if the startup winds down or undergoes a dissolution.

Preferred Vs. Participation

Liquidation preference falls into two categories: preferred and participation. The preferred category follows the rule that the original investor receives the identified multiple of the investment, per share, before founders even consider common stock. With this option, you must convert your preferred stock to common stock to receive greater payouts. When you convert to common stock, you lose your preferential treatment allowed through the holding of preferred stock. For example, preferred stock sometimes includes the issuing of dividends to shareholders.

Ross' Lesson: don't invest in startups for small dividends. Rather, you should be shooting for the unicorns that will bring 100x returns.

On the other hand, the participation category allows for the payment of the liquidation preference to Series A investors before distributing the remaining assets proportionately to common stock holders and investors alike. Since preferred stock grants more control and rights to investors, you will likely benefit from choosing that category over participation.

Negotiating for Your Ideal Preference

At the height of the investment frenzy in the early 2000s, a 10x liquidation preference did not cause startup founders to bat an eye, even though it left little for their own pockets after investors received their payouts. Today, since the market has calmed down, it is much more common to see 1x, 2x or even 3x liquidity preferences listed on term sheets and purchase agreements. These reasonable payout terms for the liquidity event allow startups to reap the rewards of supporting a future billion-dollar empire while ensuring investors receive a proper reward for the level of risk taken.

Ross' Lesson: 2x is the ideal liquidation preference for investors in the earliest investment rounds.

When you go through the negotiation process, you can start at a 3x liquidation preference with confidence that you are fair to yourself and the startup founders. Through negotiations, you may end up at 1x, but that's okay. You still stand to receive a tidy return on your investment without greedily taking the whole lot for yourself.

The Investors' Rights: What Matters

Pay attention to the section of the term sheet that relates to the rights you will receive as an investor in the startup. These rights allow you to better understand the protective provisions, participation rates, registration rights and other elements that protect your interests as an investor. Most importantly, the rights tell you what to expect to happen when the startup structure and valuation changes. If, or when, the startup experiences a liquidity event, the rights section will tell you how your shares will be handled and paid out to investors.

The standard investor rights on the term sheet are quite sufficient in protecting your interests, but there is always room for negotiation if you feel the need. Through you might be better off using the five following tactics to ensure you, and the startup founders, get the best deal:

Ross' 5 Smart Rules to Help Entrepreneurs and Investors Secure the Best Deal

1. Utilize a 30 Days or Less Policy.

Before you hand over a check to the startup founders, you must conduct your due diligence to ensure you are receiving the absolute best terms of the investment deal. The startup founders must also ensure that they are not giving up too much equity in their company.

For the mutual benefit of both parties, the decision-making process needs to happen within 30 days to avoid leaving either side wondering about the outcome. However, don't be hasty; you should never make a decision in less than a week. Give yourself time to review the terms and weigh your options before diving into the purchase agreement signing process.

2. Bring Value to All Negotiations.

Although it is expected that startups bring their winning MVP and automated delivery system – and investors bring their checkbooks, the negotiation process opens up the opportunity for even more value than that. When coming to the negotiation table, startups must offer an extraordinary opportunity to their potential investors while explaining the structure, control, and economics of the deal in the simplest terms.

Ross' Lesson: investors should go above and beyond just writing a check. For example, you should use your network to help the startup expand and find new customers.

Investors should offer not only monetary backing in the form of investing capital but also act as thought leaders and mentors to the startup founders. When everyone brings value to the negotiation table, both parties can walk away satisfied with the deal.

3. Sign the Deal and Step Back.

Once the deal is signed, and the check is written, you should not micromanage the startup in an effort to control their trajectory. Instead, you should step back and let them work their magic as they focus on the people, product, process, traction, and financials for their organization.

4. Maintain Regular Updates.

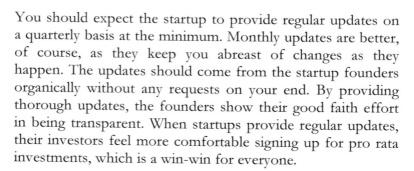

You should expect the startup to provide regular updates on a quarterly basis at the minimum. Monthly updates are better, of course, as they keep you abreast of changes as they happen. The updates should come from the startup founders organically without any requests on your end. By providing thorough updates, the founders show their good faith effort in being transparent. When startups provide regular updates, their investors feel more comfortable signing up for pro rata investments, which is a win-win for everyone.

The following is an **excellent example** of a

Hi Ross,

I hope everything is going well for you during this holiday season!

I'm happy to share our results for November along with a few other upda

template

	November 2017	Monthly Change	October 2017	Annual Change	November 2016
MRR	$1,367,200	+1.79%	$1,343,220	+32.42%	$1,032,497
ARR	$16,406,400	+1.79%	$16,118,640	+32.42%	$12,389,964
Product					
Customers	78,496	+1.18%	77,579	+21.28%	64,723
Churn Rate	5.26%	-1.50%	5.34%	+4.57%	5.03%
Net Promoter Score	52	+1.96%	51	-7.14%	56
Product Efficiency					
Revenue per Customer	$17.42	+0.60%	$17.31	+9.18%	$15.95
Lifetime Value	$331.13	+2.13%	$324.24	+4.41%	$317.15
Customer Acquisition Cost	$32.79	-2.47%	$33.62	N/A	N/A
Company Health					
Team Size	69	-2.82%	71	-12.66%	79
Revenue per Employee	$237,774	+4.74%	$227,023	+51.61%	$156,835
Bank Balance	$5,211,039	+7.54%	$4,845,897	+181.72%	$1,849,710
Gross Margin	87.85%	-0.06%	87.90%	+1.14%	86.86%
EBITDA Margin	28.27%	+4.32%	27.10%	+184.12%	9.95%

As shared last month, we've welcomed Purpose Ventures as our newest investor, as they completed a transaction purchasing a small portion of Leo's stock.

I want to share that Leo has recently decided to resign from the board, effective last week. I have full respect for his position here, and will follow up with relevant updates as and when we have them.

Finally, we've been working extensively with Buffer's legal counsel for some time now to structure a liquidity opportunity for Series A investors interested in participating in a repurchase / early redemption. If you hold Series A stock, I will be in touch when the details are finalized, to allow you to make a decision on the liquidity opportunity. For other investors, the Series A redemption will allow Buffer to structure liquidity options in the future.

I'll follow up in January with our year-end financial update and a general update on our progress and vision for 2018.

- Joel

Above are metrics from Buffer from the end of November 2017. This is real proof of how a startup should communicate with their investors after receiving a check.

Skip the Attorneys.

Attorney fees are unnecessary and burdensome for founders trying to establish and grow their startup. Often, investors can spare the funds for attorney fees, but their dollars are better spent as capital for their startup investments. As you apply every step of the Blankenship Valuation Method, and go into your negotiations well-informed, you can rest assured that your due diligence provides just as much value as an attorney's services would – and at a fraction of the price.

Ross' Lesson: instead of paying for expensive attorneys, download documents on our website at Angelkings.com/Advisors

The End Game: Shareholder and Subscription Agreements

By now you have reviewed the term sheet and feel confident about the potential for great returns, so now it is time to complete the deal by signing the shareholder and subscription agreement. These collective documents are best known as the "Stock Purchase Agreement."

1. The purchase agreement should mirror the content agreed upon in the previous non-binding term sheet. However, this time, the agreement is binding and acts as a final stamp of approval confirming your intent to invest in the startup.

2. That does not mean that you should simply gloss over the document and pen your name on the signature line; you must fully review the purchase agreement in

detail to note and rectify discrepancies between the two documents. During your review, make sure to look at the purchase price for securities to verify that the figures match your expectations.

3. Then move onto the Representation and Warranties section, which includes legally binding disclosures from the startup for your review. These disclosures detail past and future information that may sway your investment decision.

STOCK PURCHASE AGREEMENT

Representations and Warranties:	Standard representations and warranties by the Company. [Representations and warranties by Founders regarding technology ownership, etc.].[16]

[16]   Founders' representations are controversial and may elicit significant resistance as they are found in a minority of venture deals. They are more likely to appear if Founders are receiving liquidity from the transaction, or if there is heightened concern over intellectual property (e.g., the Company is a spin-out from an academic institution or the Founder was formerly with another company whose business could be deemed competitive with the Company), or in international deals. Founders' representations are even less common in subsequent rounds, where risk is viewed as

4. As you continue browsing through the purchase agreement, you will see the overall management of the corporation, including the board of director size and composition, covenants of the corporation, investor rights and procedural matters, such as the frequency of board meetings.

Board of Directors:	At the initial Closing, the Board shall consist of [____] members comprised of (i) [name] as [the representative designated by [____], as the lead Investor, (ii) [name] as the representative designated by the remaining Investors, (iii) [name] as the representative designated by the Founders, (iv) the person then serving as the Chief Executive Officer of the Company, and (v) [____] person(s) who are not employed by the Company and who are mutually acceptable [to the Founders and Investors][to the other directors].

5. Within the Representations and Warranties you should notice a line about liability insu the officers, which serves to protect y

repercussions due to lawsuits and other undesirable situations.

3. <u>Representations and Warranties of the Founders</u>. Except as set forth on the Disclosure Schedule, each of the Founders, severally and not jointly, represents and warrants to each Purchaser as of the date of the Closing at which such Purchaser is purchasing Shares as follows [(it being understood and agreed that any Founder's liability for breaches of any provisions of this <u>Section 3</u> shall be limited to the then current fair market value [as determined in good faith by the board of directors of the Company] of the shares of Common Stock of the Company currently owned by such Founder and such Founder [may, in his sole discretion, discharge such liability by the surrender of such shares or the payment of cash[63]] [shall discharge such liability by the surrender of such shares] and will terminate on the earlier of (i) [one (1) year/two (2) years] after the date of this Agreement, or (ii) the completion of an initial public offering of the Company's Common Stock)]:

6. Finally, the agreement will disclose the obligations and restrictions relating to the transfer of shares in case of death of investors and provisions for dispute resolutions between shareholders.

What Comes After Signing the Stock Purchase Agreement?

Once you sign the purchase agreement, you agree to all the listed terms and commit to providing your investment capital to the startup in exchange for the securities listed on this binding document. As this agreement is legally binding, you cannot back out after signing. You must follow through on your end of the deal, for better or worse.

Term Sheet vs. Subscription Purchase Agreement

Despite these two documents containing similar content, your due diligence depends on the thorough review of both before committing to the investment.

When you look at the purchase agreement, before signing, pay close attention to the warranties and indemnification section. The warranties will disclose any information that could impact your role as an investor or impede the success of the startup in any way. Indemnification provides a level of immunity from lawsuits to ensure you can act as an investor without worry about legal ramifications due to the startup's actions.

Unlike with the term sheet, signing the purchase agreement closes the deal and commits you as an investor for that startup. At this point, you will not have any more opportunities to negotiate a better deal or change the terms. The signed purchase agreement will also act as proof of your held shares as the company is not likely to issue actual stock certificates - this is an antiquated practice that no longer happens.

An Exploration of Convertible Notes and Their Role in Startup Success

As you move forward as a startup investor, you may encounter a document called "convertible notes." Understanding the purpose of these notes, and the caveats in their usage, will help you better approach your next investment.

Convertible notes act as a loan that turns into equity in the next round of investment funding. These notes come up most often in seed rounds by startups unsure about their valuation or other metrics usually required to attract committed investors. The convertible notes are beneficial to startups in that they receive funds immediately to use as capital without having to determine the value of their shares until a later investment round.

Investors in convertible notes can also benefit by acquiring equity at a discount within future rounds. One of the most important concepts in a convertible note is the "discount rate."

For the discount rate, if you use convertible notes at the seed round, you can expect your funds to convert into shares at a discount of the Series A price point. For example, if you agreed to a 20% discount rate, and the shares are valued at $1 per share, then your equity rate will equal $0.80 per share and allow you to secure up to 25% more overall shares in the next round.

20% discount rate valued at $1/share

=

$0.80/share allowing investors to receive 25% more shares in the future

The valuation cap is the maximum valuation an investor will convert their investment into shares. The valuation cap establishes a maximum price at which your loans convert into equity. If you sign on with a $4 million cap, and Series A valuation comes in at $1 per share with an $8 million dollar valuation, then you receive equity at the lower price of $0.50 a share.

Valuation Cap

You invest at at $4 million-dollar cap

The Series A valuation is at $1 per share at an $8 million-dollar valuation

Then you receive equity at $0.50 per share

Since convertible notes are a form of loans, they come with an interest rate attached, but that is not the reason you should investing. You should be investing in startups to receive 100x returns, not to profit on high interest rates.

Your loan to the startup has a maturity date as well, so you can receive repayment from the founders within a certain time period. And always remember, there is a risk of insolvency as the return of loan money is *never* guaranteed.

Ross' Lesson: don't invest in startups just to receive interest as a loan. Invest to hit a grand slam home run!

Knowledge is Power

With the right knowledge on your side, you can head into investments with confidence, knowing you performed your due diligence. Although you are never guaranteed success, the

Blankenship Valuation Method and supporting documentation, are there to help you receive large returns on your investments. Knowing what you know now, you will never go into a deal blind and misinformed. Now you can assess the level of risk and make a calculated decision by knowing how the economics and control factors influence the potential success of each startup you consider backing.

8

Conclusion

"Everyone here has the sense that right now is one of those moments when we are influencing the future."

-Steve Jobs

This is not the end, but rather the beginning of what will be a successful, profitable lifetime for you as an angel investor or venture capitalist. You might even want to start your own company after reading this book!

Whether you go part-time, full-time or absolutely all-in with the new tools and formula you've learned in this book, you're now at a perfect inflection point for real change in your life.

Stop sitting on the sidelines with regret, listening to stories of others who found and invested in the next billion-dollar companies.

There will always be another bite at the apple. And that apple may just be discovering the next "Apple Computer," before other investors get to it.

In this book, your journey began with the introduction of five new principles to investing. All of these principles are based on the **"Blankenship Valuation Method."** I now want you to use this method to not only know what you're searching for, but to establish the proper foundation and language so you can start listening better, understanding more, and simplifying the DNA that embodies every startup: *People, Product, Process, Traction and Financials.*

Here's a reminder of where the core Startup DNA of the next billion-dollar companies:

Within the **People** chapter, I explained how important it is to find and invest in those quirky ambivert founders who refused to take "No" for an answer as they were so often rejected throughout their lives.

Within the **Product** chapter, I explained how a product should be simple, sticky, and make people fall in love with the company by way of the startup's first product.

Within the **Process** chapter, I explained how most startups are neither scalable nor automated from day one. That every process is the same, whether you're dealing with an online technology or a simple iOS or Android application; and that process is rooted in the necessity for a startup to try, test and learn before building products or a process that is overly-complicated or scalable without anything worth scaling.

Within the **Traction** chapter, I explained to you how you need to "CAPTURE" the community's attention with the love and care you show for them as either customers (B2C) or businesses (B2B). Gaining traction allows a startup to tap into the human-side of buying, that you're able to create genuine rapport and relationships that turn into repeat subscribers and lifetime customers who care about your success as a startup.

Within the **Financials** chapter, I explained that investors need to know and understand financials as well as the Founders themselves. Before you ever write a check to a founder, or before a founder ever launches a "startup," knowledge will empower and increase that startup's chances of succeeding. If you want to build a billion-dollar startup - who doesn't? - then it's about knowing the data and the profit model to bring you success.

And **startups**, remember to…

Start creating your own monopoly.

Start building the best in-house Hackers, Hustlers and Growth Hackers.

Start becoming erudite thought leader who makes a difference.

And stop expecting investors to come to you without a meaningful and long-term plan to build a sustainably profitable brand name.

You are your greatest resource to begin the journey of becoming a successful investor. Just as successful startups share the same DNA, by reading this book and seeing further resources, you've proven you're ready.

Now go ahead and build, create, and learn from the endless amounts of resources that we have provided you as a starting place to get to your end goal of generating massive wealth, while changing lives and empowering others through your hard earned capital.

If you have any questions, don't hesitate to reach us directly: invest@angelkings.com

You can also learn more about Angel Kings, here (AngelKings.com/Invest).

While we currently on work with accredited investors, we always welcome your questions, comments, and concerns on your journey.

Glossary

Ambivert – Ambiverts possess a combination of both introverted and extroverted personality types. Investors should always seek ambiverts as they are the most ideal founder personalities that tend to be the most successful.

Articles of Incorporation – A set of formal documents filed with a government body to legally document the creation of a company.

Brand Culture – Brand Culture is when a company is recognized for its "brand name" and has a community of evangelical followers who are interested in that company and its products.

BUILD – An acronym that explains potential problems startups may face as they build their founding team and expand by hiring new employees.

Bylaws and Board of Directors' Documents – A set of documents that cover the name of the company, founding members, the Board of Directors, committee type, officers, meetings, conflicts of interest and amendments.

CAPTURE – An acronym explaining how the presence of a great process allows for a company to gain traction, which will ultimately have a positive impact on the growth of a startup.

Convertible Notes – Convertible notes are structured as loans with the intention of converting the loan into equity.

Economics & Control – The economics of a deal involve the amount of capital invested and what percentage of the company the investor receives as a result of his or her investment. Control refers to who is in charge of the startup throughout its life cycle and subsequent rounds of investment. Control also relates to what investor rights' one receives by way of his or her investment.

ELEVATOR – An acronym that helps determine whether a startup's product can become a successful brand name.

Growth Hacker – The Growth Hacker is a storyteller who can craft a good narrative for the company and tell that story to the general public through the use of social media and the Internet.

Hacker – The Hacker is the core engineer, responsible for coding and building the product.

Hustler – The Hustler's main focus is to bring in many customers in the most cost-effective way possible

IRS Employer Identification Number "EIN" – The IRS Identification Number is used to identify a business entity and is also known as a Federal Tax Identification Number.

Lifetime Value (LTV) – The Lifetime Value - or known as the Lifetime Customer Value - is a prediction of the net profit attributed to one customer over the course of a startup's existence.

Liquidation Preference – The liquidation preference determines the payout order in a liquidation event, such as the sale of the company.

Minimum Viable Product (MVP) – The MVP is a functioning demo of a product that provides meaningful value to a customer in demonstrably fast time.

Open-sharing phenomenon – The strategy used by startups that allows its customers (Netflix and Facebook examples) to share product logins and code, without blocking these customers or creating obstacles to their enjoyment.

Option Pool – An option pool is when stock is set aside so it can be given to employees in the future.

PACED – An acronym that describes characteristics (Passionate, Ambivert, Calculated Risk Taker, Erudite, and Dedicated) of the most successful, billion-dollar founders.

Subscription Purchase Agreement – The Subscription Purchase Agreement is an official document that outlines the *binding* terms for a company selling shares to an investors at a certain price, in exchange for equity and control in the company.

Term Sheet – A non-binding document that provides the foundation for startup founders and investors to negotiate an investment at any round.

Total Addressable Market (TAM) – The size of the entire industry and what startups hope to dominate.

X-Factor – A noteworthy, special quality that makes a product unique and better than the products already on the market.

ABOUT ROSS D. BLANKENSHIP

Ross D. Blankenship ("The Investing King") is a successful entrepreneur, investor and advisor in America's top startups.

After graduating from Cornell University and then Washington University School of Law, Blankenship has become a leading consultant for companies with challenges such as capital fundraising, operations, and business restructuring. Blankenship continues to build great companies across America and around the world.

Blankenship is available for interview, speaking, and advisor requests by contacting directly (invest@angelkings.com).

why not interview all living authors?!

Made in the USA
Columbia, SC
18 September 2019